Of Moose and Men

A skewed look at life in Alaska

II

Of Moose and Men
A skewed look at life in Alaska

by
A. E. Poynor

Foreword by Donnis Thompson, Kenai Peninsula Homesteader

OMM Books
Nikiski, Alaska

OMM Books
P.O. Box 7397
Nikiski, Alaska 99635

ISBN 0-9667915-0-9

This book was printed and manufactured in the U.S.A.

Cover art and design by:
mARTy at The Frontier Frame Gallery, Soldotna, Alaska

Dedication

This book is dedicated to those who helped to write it

by being themselves: friends and family.

I promise not to tell who is who.

About the Author

A. E. Poynor was born in Michigan, and lived in other various places while growing up such as: Illinois, Missouri, Arizona and New Mexico. He first dragged his wife and daughter to Alaska, in 1976, on an all-expenses-paid, three year tour with the U.S. Army. During those three years, the family grew to four, with the addition of a son, and Alaska got into his blood.

Described as, "One of the dumbest things I could have done... aside from urinating on an electric fence," he left Alaska to attend school following his discharge. Five years passed before he and the family made it back to Alaska.

The Poynors have lived on the Kenai Peninsula since 1984, and now only leave Alaska for very short periods of time, to visit relatives in the Lower Forty-eight.

Contents

Foreword

Alan has written some very funny commentaries in this book about contemporary Alaskans. For reasons unkown to normal people, he decided the foreword should be written by an old homesteader. So...

"Back in the 50's..." (or 40's) as we crusty old homesteaders like to say, things were mighty tough. The winters were far colder. There was no electricity on the homestead. There was little money, and few jobs. Homesteads were not "free," they were costly. A home had to be built and lived in. Land had to be cleared to fulfill the regulations of the BLM in order to "prove up" because the rules were essentially the same ones that applied during the Oklahoma land rush. We were supposed to clear and plant so that we could farm. Problem was that little would grow here in the way of crops. Potatoes did fine, but it was hard to sell to each other and, after the space under the bed in the tiny cabin was full, where else could one store unsold spuds?

It is fashionable nowadays to presume homesteading was a real kick, a rural vacation (as many things look through the crooked glass of nostalgia), but the fact was that many folks literally starved out, and many did not, could not, prove up and they had to move and leave their labors, their hoped-for land, and their dreams.

It's true there were compensations and rewards, but I didn't realize at the time, as I packed wood and carried water, how humorous it all was. It took a doggoned cheechako (Well, what else do you call a person who has only lived here a mere 15 years?) to point out to me our Alaskan foibles.

It occurs to me that Alan knows entirely too much about human nature, and therefore, very likely presents a danger to us all. We'll see.

In the meantime, enjoy the stories.

Donnis Thompson
A very old homesteader

Looking Like a *Real* Alaskan

Last June, under protest, because summer is the reward Alaskans receive for making it through winter, I found myself in Arizona visiting family. I was introduced to my parents' neighbor one night. Upon learning I was from Alaska, she looked me over critically, then said, "You don't look like a *real* Alaskan."

Up to that point, my thoughts had been primarily centered around how I was going to extricate myself from the plastic lawn chair I was sitting in without: a) producing a disgusting noise, b) leaving behind the skin from the back of my legs, or c) both of the above.

Her question redirected my thoughts. What is a *real* Alaskan supposed to look like? Obviously, there must be certain things that conjure up the image. I ran through the times that I had seen someone and thought, "Oooo... there goes a *real* Alaskan," and prioritized them.

First off, a *real* Alaskan has to have lots of facial hair. This isn't a requirement placed on the females in the state, but I've known some who look the part. The bigger and bushier the beard, the more Alaskan you are. Good mutton chop sideburns, graced with a full curl handlebar mustache, are an acceptable substitute. Beards should be full and thick enough to support a two ounce piece of moose steak, dropped off a fork, from a height of one-half inch above the lower lip. Mustaches must be long enough to strain bugs, spruce needles and other outdoors stuff from your drinking cup.

Shirts are almost as important. A *real* Alaskan owns an endless supply of plaid shirts-- all of them ugly. Wool is probably the favorite material, as it will shrink to ill-fitting shapes, and holds a good wrinkle. Cotton flannel comes in a close second due to its ability to stain easily, but doesn't itch nearly enough. Also, cotton flannel will lose a good wrinkle with just a few short days of wear. I suppose a *real* Alaskan might wear a solid colored chamois shirt, but only if the tails were short enough to come untucked by themselves.

Women are at a distinct advantage when it comes to plaid shirts. They have a much greater selection of ugly plaid colors to choose from, as compared to the few basic ugly colors men have. As a matter of fact, the very best *real* Alaskan shirt I've ever seen was a woman's. It was a yellow with gray plaid, highlighted beautifully with blotchy stains from salmon blood. The owner had, at one time, dried it too close to the wood stove, resulting in a scorched left sleeve that was much shorter than the right. So much so, the sleeve couldn't be buttoned. It was truly a masterpiece.

Real Alaskans don't wear anything as simple as hats. They wear headgear. It must do more than cover your head, it must make a statement. The statement is, "I don't care how silly I look, as long as I'm warm." The best headgear is made from fur, preferably something with a face and a tail (headgear from beaver being the exception). Very short foxes are in great demand. When the very finest headgear is worn, a REAL Alaskan looks like they've been attacked by a misguided, amorous Pomeranian.

Real Alaskans wear only brown cotton duck work pants. They must be faded, have shredded cuffs, and at least two holes caused by chainsaw mishaps. The proper *real* Alaskan would pale at the thought of mismatched, brown cotton duck work pants and an ugly plaid shirt, so the stains must be of a common origin. Example: salmon slime stains would be acceptable with outboard motor grease.

Brown cotton duck work pants can be held in place with either suspenders or a belt and knife. *Real* Alaskans hold their suspenders in reserve for formal occasions such as Fur Rendezvous, the Cordova Iceworm Festival or the Seward Silver Salmon Derby. The suspenders must be wide, brightly colored and actually hold the pants up. They cannot just dangle ornamentally at the sides, or they will become entangled with fishing gear. For everyday wear, a belt and knife are in order. The belt can be of any material, but old, limp leather is best. It can be tooled, but can't have a name on it unless the name is preceded by a town name. Example: "Kenai-Kate" or "Sitka-Sam." For obvious reasons, belts with names on them are not common in Tuntutuliak. When belts are worn, they must be held in place with a filet knife.

To finish out the *real* Alaskan look, shoes, or worse yet, footwear must be shunned. Only boots will suffice: hip boots, hiking boots, work boots, any boot but cowboy boot. The color, style or brand doesn't matter, as long as they are heavy. The best rule of thumb I've heard came from an old homesteader in Nikiski, "If it don't weigh at least five pounds, it ain't a boot. It's a slipper."

So that's what *real* Alaskans look like. And to Mrs. Peevish of Phoenix, Arizona: I'm sorry, it was just too damn hot.

Moose Confusion

Upon visiting Alaska, one priority usually set is having a moose experience. The largest of the deer family, the moose seems to embody the frontier life. Each person arrives with a preconceived notion of the moose. What a noble animal. What an awe inspiring creature. What an example of grandeur personified. Then the truth: what a disappointment.

"Martha, that can't be a moose. I think it's a sick horse with rheumatoid withers."

"It is so a moose... And oh, look! It has a baby! No! *Twins.* Oh Alfie, they're *so* cute. Get a picture. Get a picture."

Ninety-nine percent of the time, only a small instant camera is available. One that automatically focuses and reduces any subject to a small, indiscernible, brown dot. Most owners know about the reduce to an indiscernible brown dot feature on their cameras after the first roll is developed, so our photographer climbs out of the safety of his vehicle to stalk the perfect shot. He is coached from the car.

"Get closer, dear. You don't want any of those indiscernible brown dots again. Get Closer!"

Our photographer is concentrating. He is lost in the pursuit of his art. Totally absorbed, he hasn't noticed that the calves have been slowly angling back toward the cow, whose ears are laid back upon lowered head. Closing in slowly, inching his way along, using every fiber of woodland skill learned from life in suburbia, Alfie discovers there are now three moose in the viewfinder. One is very large and very menacing.

Adrenaline takes over the actions of all parties concerned. Our photographer stands bolt upright from his crouched position. The moose see the aggressive stance, and react instinctively: they whirl and assume their basic camera defense position, the Moose-moon. Not an ordinary single, or the less common double, but the full-blown, up close and personal, triple-whammy moose moon! With the simple press of a button, Alfie and Martha become the envy of all their neighbors. (Although it will be awfully hard to convince the folks back home, "That's the moose that almost charged.")

How is it that moose know just the right moment to turn? Scientists believe that animals have an innate ability for telepathic communication. Along that line, I believe humans have a similar innate ability, but ours is restricted to sending the message, "I will now push the button on my camera." I have done considerable research on this subject. An entire photo album at home is dedicated to moose moons. The album is handy when visitors outstay their welcome, "Oh yeah, this one had at least a sixty inch rack. It's on the end in the bushes."

Visitors to the Greatland have only this one indignity to endure. Those of us who live here year-round have to tolerate additional forms of moose shenanigans.

Adolescent moose have no more concept of their mortality than do their human counterparts. This leads them into an area of common fascination: the automobile. Young moose love to play around roads. Game biologists would have you believe it is to feed on the vegetation growing alongside the road, but the real truth is that they are looking for a good game of "Panic Stop."

The game consists of two or more young moose just fooling around by the road. At the approach of a vehicle, all but one hides in the bushes. The one youngster left to play the game waits until the right moment to step out in front of the vehicle, causing the driver to "Panic Stop." It's not hard to imagine the other moose in the bushes snickering and giggling at the expression on the driver's face. It's all great sport, and everyone enjoys it immensely, except the driver. The object of the game is to see how close the car can get without actually hitting the player. Generally, the winner gets first pick in the nearest vegetable garden.

As moose grow older and heavier, they resort to less perilous pastimes. One of the best known is "Divot." This game is mostly limited to the wet seasons, and requires a well-groomed, or better still, newly planted lawn. The object is to prance across the lawn, gouging large holes with every step. A good size player can leave a hole large enough to swallow small children or lawn-mowers, but even a minor leaguer can at least cripple a jogger or two. The worst aspect of this game is that nothing will ever grow in the hole again. The soil becomes poisoned, and trying to fill in the holes is an exercise in futility. Golfers in Alaska soon learn to check every moose divot they stumble over, much as a kid checks the coin return slots on vending machines. If two or more moose compete at "Divot," the winner gets first pick at a nearby vegetable garden.

"Shadowing" is a game moose play from October to March, between the hours of six-thirty and eight o'clock in the morning. It requires at least one-half mile of remote road, bordered by thick vegetation, and a small child between the ages of five and ten, on the way to a bus stop. The object is to get the child to break into a dead run before reaching the bus stop. As the child leaves the house, the moose follows, unseen, inside the tree line. The moose makes just enough noise to catch the child's attention. As the pace quickens, snapping a limb from a tree will generally produce a trot from the child. A loud snort anytime after that will elicit a shriek and a full run. All of this must be accomplished without being seen, or the player is disqualified. If the child is too encumbered with clothing to work up to a full head of steam, the moose will resort to the "dash and stomp finale." This is performed by passing the child, while still unseen in the trees, with as much noise as possible, then bursting out onto the road, stomping and snorting. The resultant wails of stark terror are music to the moose's ears, but the best part seems to be watching the scattered homework drift down from the heavens. If two or more moose compete in this game, the winner gets dibs on any nearby, expensive, exotic shrubbery.

Dogs frequently become the brunt of moose games. Tied dogs are a temptation few moose can pass up. "Doggin' it" equates fun and games for moose. Staying out of sight, the moose works itself into an upwind position from the dog. The dog responds by barking and carrying on. The dog's owner responds by stepping out and verbally abusing the dog. If played with finesse the dog is reduced to a slavering bundle of nerves, and the owner resembles a cuckoo, poking out every fifteen minutes shouting, "Shut-up!"

If the dog's owner isn't home, "Tetherdog" can be played. In this game, the moose stands just outside of the dog's reach, and slowly circles the dog while nonchalantly nibbling on a prized shrub or two. Soon enough, the dog's chain is wrapped tightly around the stake. When the dog can utter no more than a wheezy squeak, the game is over. If two or more moose play this game, the winner gets first pick at the nearest vegetable garden, as the exotic and expensive bushes are, no doubt, gone.

As if all the above were not enough, there exists one more game moose play to make life miserable for the humans in their domain. "Peek-a-moose" is a rather innocuous name for what amounts to the Superbowl of moosefoolery. As near as I can figure it, Peek-a-moose is how moose get even with homeowners that don't plant enough expensive, exotic shrubbery. The game is simple. The moose hides around a corner of the house, waiting for some unsuspecting individual to step outside and approach the hiding spot. When the victim reaches a distance of no more than two feet from the hiding spot, the moose jumps out and snorts: Peek-a-moose! The chaos that results from this sudden appearance resembles a disorganized Chinese fire drill, as arms and legs flail wildly in the attempt to return to the door. If it's the moose's lucky day, there are several people walking in line, and it will be hours before all the arms and legs are disentangled.

Meanwhile, the moose trots off, past the vegetable garden that has recently been laid to waste, almost stepping on the whimpering, huddled dog. That moose has had a particularly good day.

Whoee Doggies

Alaskans are, as a rule, fond of dogs. Some say that it's a holdover from the days when sled dogs were a primary means of transportation. Mostly, I think it's that we just don't know any better, or have masochistic tendencies.

A good dog is a friend, a protector, a constant companion, and usually a continual source of aggravation. Size is of the utmost importance to qualify as a good dog in Alaska. Those motile little balls of hair that sound like broken whoopee cushions when stepped on in the dark, don't count. We are thinking *DAWG* here. The bigger the better. The best Alaskan dogs are of dubious lineage with a little Husky thrown in to allow claims of part wolf.

The size of a good dog precipitates problems. Food is the first that comes to mind. It's not bad enough that huge dogs require huge amounts of money for huge amounts of food, but those huge amounts of food have to be transported and stored. I have single-handedly caused an entire shift of bagboys to quit at the local grocery by casually asking the checker if there were limits to the latest sale on dog food.

Transportation and storage problems can be solved together in the winter. I simply keep the bags in the back of the truck. When I start sliding off the road on a regular basis, it's time to buy more. It's a different story in the summer though, as a single seventy-five pound bag of dry dog food will absorb enough water to surpass the axle rating. The food must be stored in a covered area.

Since I want to feed only my valuable cur, and not bears or the neighbors' worthless mutts, storage means in the house. When we were first married, and our home was decorated in a shipping crate and line spool motif, my wife didn't mind. However, amazing inroads have been made in civilizing me over the past seventeen years, and even I can see that Early American and Modern Purina don't compliment one another.

By draping a woven rag rug over the bags, two things are accomplished: first, the bags are obscured from view, and secondly, when visitors try to smooth the lumps out of the rug, I know it's time to buy more food.

If only the food was kept inside, dog ownership would be easy. But with a soft-hearted wife and two kids, the dog comes inside too. So do a myriad of difficulties. Barfing is one of them.

When any other animal on the face of the planet doesn't feel good, it quits eating. Not so with a dog. What is the first thing a dog does when it feels sick? It stuffs itself as full of grass and other foreign material as possible, and then comes in to eat a full bowl of dog food. This is tantamount to a human with the stomach flu getting more than their money's worth at an all you can eat sauerkraut and barbecue ribs buffet.

The big difference is, the human would have sense enough to be sick and get it over with. Again, not so with a dog. Dogs have to work up to being sick so that everyone within earshot will know. They take delight in generating a gag reflex. If you want to witness the definition of pandemonium, go to the average home with tan carpeting and watch what happens when any dog starts going, "Haarrumfa!"

It would be bad enough if a dog did this at a civilized hour, but they always wait until late at night. Now, let's compound the situation with a good dog. Butcher, the large wonder dog, starts his gag reflex serenade. Instantly, everyone in the house screams, "Where's the dog?" This is a really stupid question. The dog is going to be as far away from an outside door as possible. That is a given. So is the fact that being a good dog, Butcher is too darn big to pick up. So Dad dashes to the door in just his underwear, dances out onto the porch, whistling and clapping his hands while hopping around in bare feet, as a shrill winter wind screams from the north.

Butcher, distracted by all the commotion, stops gagging long enough to check out just what the hell is going on. The dog is forced to spend a quiet fifteen to thirty minutes outside before being allowed to return inside to repeat the whole process. The process may be repeated, with the dog going in and out several times to no avail. There *will* be a stain on the carpet before morning.

Another problem: dogs shed hair. A good dog is going to weigh at least a hundred-twenty pounds, half of which is hair. Most of that hair will find its way to the floor in the spring. The prelude to the shedding season is a uniform coating of dog hair on your floor. It comes on slowly, and you don't really notice it until a visiting friend comments on your nice Angora socks when you're actually bare-footed. Whereas someone down South with their thin coated dog will occasionally find a hair on the floor, at the peak of shedding season, the proud Alaskan dog owner will trip over hunks of hair the size and weight of a bowling ball.

Shedding season forces the dog back outside, where the owner will encounter a veritable Pandora's Box of other problems. The most immediate of which is an accumulation of "doggie blossoms" that crop up in the receding snow. This doesn't bother me in the least. I have a son. It was originally easy to convince him that it was just like looking for Easter eggs with a shovel. We have now moved on to the bounty system: he gets a nickel for each blossom. Even at a moderate inflation rate, it will soon cost more to recover the dog food than it did to originally purchase it.

Other things start to reappear as the melt continues, like the old moose that disappeared in February. You can stake your life on the fact that Butcher knows exactly where that moose laid down for the final time. Now that the sun is out, and the days are warmer, he's going to pay his respects. That is, after he checks out where the neighbors threw the leftover fish from their spring freezer cleaning. No dog ever had it so good. And no dog ever smelled so grand. It's so... so heady, so piquant, so disgustingly awful, he can hardly wait to get home and share it.

Up he bounds, lost in a scent-induced state of euphoria, panting that putrid fishy breath, high on life and the fumes of decom-position. The unwitting owner reaches down to pat the faithful beast, and recoils upon feeling the malodorous coating. Too late.

Amputation is the only sure way to remove the odor from the owner.

The stench is typically so bad that the dog is given a wide berth instead of a bath for a few days. This is much to the dog's liking, as he can come and go as he pleases. During this time, there are only two kinds of animals that get near the pungent canine-- other dogs, because they want to compare rancidity, and porcupines, because they are slow.

Porcupines don't have "Kick Me" signs on them, but that's okay. Dogs can't read. Dogs perceive porcupines as the geeks of the animal world. Once a dog has spotted a porcupine, he will not rest until he's sporting a face full of quills. A dog won't have just one encounter with a porcupine. It seems that after the first loss, dogs spend the rest of their lives trying to even the score. Once, in the short span of just three weeks, my dog tangled with the neighborhood porcupine four times. I suspect the dog's strategy was to eventually strip the porcy naked so that it would freeze to death.

Most dog owners in this neck of the woods have stepped out onto the porch to find their dog doing an imitation of a drooling, foul smelling, natural bristle brush. There are only two ways to handle the situation: either take the dog to the vet, or try and pull the quills yourself, and then take the dog to the vet.

A trip to the vet will always be more expensive for the owner of a good dog. Any procedure seems to call for sedation when a large dog is involved. For a while, I thought my vet charged by the pound for treating animals. His first words are always, "Ah yes. And what does Butcher weigh now?"

I can appreciate why a vet would want to sedate a big dog before working on it. What I don't appreciate is the order to "keep him quiet for twenty-four hours." Hell, if I could have kept him quiet for just five minutes, I wouldn't have needed to take him to the vet in the first place.

Confinement doesn't set well with good dogs. They are into the freewheelin' kind of lifestyle. Fences are a good idea, until the snow piles up. At that point, fences become strictly a symbolic thing. Dogs don't do well with symbolism. They need a solid, tangible means to define their confinement. A heavy chain and stout stake fill the requirements perfectly.

The only problem with chaining a good dog is that the effect is similar to condensing a demolition derby into a fifty foot circle. Even the dumbest mutt quickly learns that running about gleefully results in abrupt and unpleasant stops. The dog must resort to a stationary exercise program: digging. Digging is to dogs, what running in place and flapping arms is to Jane Fonda. And no matter what your personal view may be of Ms. Fonda, at least she doesn't tear up the carpet and scratch through the floor. A chained dog can, in very short order, turn a section of lawn into an excellent imitation of an artillery impact zone.

Yes indeed, I know I'm fond of dogs. When I sit and look at ol' Butcher, peering over the dog food bags, past the spotted and fuzzy carpet, out onto what looks like a strip mining operation, there is no question of my fondness. My intelligence is another matter.

14

Mudrooms

Homes in different regions of the country have distinctive characteristics or design criteria that will set them apart from homes in other portions of the country. Back East, it's the foyer. People don't have front halls, they have foyers. This lends an aura of dignity when someone comes visiting, "Oh, how lovely! Dried out weeds bundled all together in a wrinkled bow. It will go perfectly in the *foi-yay*. I'm trying to maintain a welcoming country motif in here."

In the Southwest, I was recently told, all the rage in home construction is the lanai: a living room that opens out onto the back porch or veranda. What is a Hawaiian room doing in the desert? I don't know. Why aren't those rooms called "Southwest rooms?" Perhaps there is some fear of confusing the builders.

"Jake, if this don't beat all I ever seen. Right here on the plans for this house it says 'Southwest room.' Well, any dang fool can see it's gonna be in the northeast corner of the house! Say, you don't suppose we got the wrong plans here, do ya?"

"Naw, just flip the sheet over."

I heard from a relative that the big thing in the central part of the country is the "bay" window. If you're going to build a house worth keeping, you've got to have a bay window. Presumably, the bay window was a design that allowed the families of eastern seafarers the opportunity to keep watch for their loved one's safe return. That makes sense, but really now, what is someone in the plains states going to do with a bay window? Are they supposed to wait for dad to drive up in the old prairie schooner after a hard day at the office?

Alaskans are more practical and descriptive in their approach to naming the portion of their homes that distinguishes them as an Alaskan domicile. We have the "mudroom."

The mudroom is a wonderful attachment to what might just be any home in the Lower Forty-eight. They appear to have been hung on the front of the house as a partially completed afterthought. Generally constructed only of the finest quality, unpainted plywood, and provided with wiring but no heat, windows or finishing touches. The mudroom stands out as Alaska's gift to the world of architecture, and falls second only to the indoor bathroom in importance to the Alaskan homeowner.

Obviously, the descriptive but ignoble name of mudroom doesn't do much to help sell houses to people unfamiliar with the phrase, so there is a more palatable term applied by real estate agents: the Arctic Entryway. That just sort of rolls off your tongue doesn't it? It looks great in print too.

"Oooh Honey, did you see this ad? It's a three bedroom, two bath, split level home with *Arctic Entryway*. Arctic Entryway. That sounds so Alaskan! Let's call the Realtor and look at it."

The romance is over upon arrival at the prospective dream home.

"Ugh, this is a disgusting little room. Looks like a mudroom. May we see the Arctic Entryway?"

The important thing to keep in mind about mudrooms is that they serve as more than just simple barriers between carpet and whatever might be tracked into the home. The mudroom plays an integral role in the daily life of an Alaskan.

The mudroom is where all the day to day items of survival are kept.

"Honey? I can't find the duct tape."

"It's on the shelf in the mudroom."

The mudroom serves as the ultimate toy box.

"Mom? Have you seen my hockey stick?"

"It's in the mudroom, behind the door."

The mudroom is the Alaskan answer to what used to be called the pantry: "Just put the dog food in the mudroom."

The mudroom is the general depot for any item needed, no matter what you want to do. Or for that matter, whatever time of the year you want to do it.

"Have you seen my snowshoes?"

"In the corner, next to the lawn chairs, behind the dog food, probably under the sleeping bags."

The mudroom can serve as the hunter's best friend.

"Gotta age this moose a little before we package it. Let's put a few hooks in the ceiling of the mudroom, and hang it there."

The mudroom is also the perfect cooler for those impromptu get togethers.

"Wanna beer? Cold ones are right out there in the mudroom."

The major problem with mudrooms is that they are never big enough to satisfy the demands placed on them. Once all the canoe paddles, snowshoes, L'il Chief Smokers, fishing rods, tackle boxes, freezers, life jackets, mauls, axes, ropes, guns, dog food bags, drinks, assorted sports equipment, power and hand tools, spare boat/auto/airplane parts, tarps, gas cans, and various pieces of exercise equipment are in place, there is hardly room for muddy shoes. I guess that would explain why, in the past few years, I have noticed a decline in the number of houses that have visible mudrooms. I guess people are opting to buy bigger homes with more storage space.

At the same time, I've noticed an increase in the number of garages that have standard house doors on them. The people that have regular car doors on their garages also seem to prefer keeping their cars outside all the time.

Could there be a connection?

Stuff

It is with some apprehension that I address this subject. The war between the sexes has been raging for as long as mankind has existed. The battlefield is strewn with the twisted and mangled bodies of men that have made casual observations on the situation.

There is something about men that attracts them to hobbies that require an accumulation of specialized equipment and supplies. This seems doubly so in Alaska. In the warmer months there are the outdoor hobbies, and in the winter there are hobbies best conducted indoors. Alaskan men have double the opportunity to collect goodies that their Lower Forty-eight counterparts do.

Any activity conducted in the outdoors requires the use of gear and equipment specially designed and constructed for ease of portability. This makes such gear and equipment less than suitable to perform the equivalent indoor task. Rugged though the gear may be, its size precludes using it for most domestic applications.

"Dear, I thought I'd make a batch of deep-fried chicken for dinner tonight. Would you please set up the pack stove?"

"Sure 'nuff, Honey. You going to make just a little, or should I dig out the big, full pint pot?"

Even hobbies that are indoor in nature require the accumulation of considerable doo-dads in order to provide maximum satisfaction. Really. How many men could be entirely satisfied with a hobby such as, for instance, bridge? Bridge is a game that a person can play for a lifetime and still never completely master, but what kind

19

of satisfaction is there to be had in a simple deck of cards? That isn't nearly enough paraphernalia to keep most men happy.

No, if a man is going to play cards as a hobby, he's going to pick something like poker. It's not that poker is any more macho, playing cards is playing cards, it's that poker requires all sorts of extra doo-dads to be done up right. Besides the cards themselves, there's the chips, and with chips, a nifty table with all the little places to store the chips while playing is necessary. Along with the special table, one might as well provide the best possible ambiance with a specially designed and decorated light to hang over the table. And of course, if going so far as to spend money on a table and a light is necessary, the least one could do is provide some special, fancy chairs for the whole shebang. Soon enough, a simple pastime takes up a major portion of at least one room.

The most common complaint Alaskan women voice about their significant other having a hobby, isn't that there's not enough time, but that there's never enough room to accommodate all the goodies.

The conflict in this situation is heightened by the fact that many women don't appreciate or recognize the importance of all the doo-dads required to achieve maximum enjoyment out of a hobby. To women, everything that is accumulated in the pursuit of relaxation and enjoyment is relegated to the generic category of *stuff.*

"Look at this room! It's a mess! You have all your *stuff* piled and scattered everywhere. What do you need all this *stuff* for anyway? You never even use most of this *stuff.*"

"Well, that's because I have to work. If I could reload, go shooting, hunt, fish and just in general fool around for a living, I'd use all this valuable equipment on a daily basis."

"You probably don't even know what half of this *stuff* is. What is this?"

"It's a rod butt. It broke off one of my ultra-light rods summer before last."

"It's *broken*! Why keep it? It's worthless."

"No, it's not. As soon as one of my medium poles breaks, I'll epoxy the tip end into the broken butt, and have a really good ice fishing rig."

"Well, can't you store it someplace out of the way? Like under the house?"

"Oh, no. If I put it under the house, I might forget I've got it, and there wouldn't have been any point in saving it."

"What are these? I thought you bought a new pair of waders last spring. Why do you keep these old ones?"

"Well, only one boot leaks. If I save them, when one of the new boots gets a leak, maybe it'll be on the opposite foot, and that way I'll still have one good pair."

"Why not throw out the leaking boot? That way, we'd only have to store one boot."

"Yeah, but if the same foot on my new pair starts leaking, then I'll use a little duct tape, and have two passable pairs."

"Why didn't you use a 'little duct tape' to begin with, and save us the sixty dollars the new pair cost?"

"No man should be without a back-up pair of waders."

Storage is the big problem with a man's hobby paraphernalia. There just is never enough room "out of the way" to accommodate proper storage. No matter where a guy puts something, it occupies a space that will be deemed to be an invaluable location by his spouse. This follows the Law of Unused Corners: any vacant corner will be completely ignored until it is put to good use storing things best left ignored. A totally useless, out of the way corner that fairly begs for something to occupy it will go completely unnoticed up until the point at which it is given a reason for existence in the form of doo-dad storage. Once the forgotten corner is put into useful service, it will immediately become the "perfect" spot for an artistic display of dried and dyed weeds or wheat stalks.

It was suggested about four years ago that the answer to the "stuff" conflict around our house would be to build a place to keep all the things necessary for the pursuit of all the various hobbies a man could have. It was a good idea, put forth in an earnest manner by my wife. That's how the concept of our extra large carport, with loft, came to be. Since building a carport was an extension of my woodworking hobby, and it offered a phenomenal opportunity to acquire some special tools, I embraced the idea wholeheartedly. With all that extra space up above the cars, everything a man might own could be stored out of the way and ready for use at a moment's notice. In fact, such an area could actually serve as a workshop, eliminating the need to carry on projects inside the house. It was a brilliant idea that presented a win-win situation.

It just might be that this is the year I get all those special tools out of the corner in the family room, and actually build the thing. On the other hand, if the carport is built, it might limit the scope of our conversations.

Foraging

Healthful, natural eating seems the new lifestyle of choice, both in terms of making sense, and in being chic. The lifestyle of cholesterol laden, rich and creamy excess is no longer considered fashionable. Gone are the days when double helpings of a thick slab of rare beef, scarfed down with a side of whipped potatoes slathered in cream gravy were the way to go. Say good-bye to heaped plates of pork roast with creamed baby potatoes and peas. Fat and flavor are out. The current fashionable way to good health is through massive consumption of plant matter. And the ultimate in health is found in eating only natural and organic plant foodstuffs.

I can think of nothing that will get you into natural and organic faster than foraging for food. With only six commonly acknow-ledged poisonous plants in Alaska, the fen and forest surrounding us could be viewed as a virtual cornucopia of good health. The world's grandest salad bar, if you will, open seven days a week, twenty-four hours a day, for over three straight months. Combine that with an "all you can stand to eat" offer, and throw in the fact that it's free. All of a sudden it doesn't sound so bad.

Frankly, I think the state tourism folks are missing a good bet here. Sums of money that rival a Spielberg production budget are spent to produce primetime television ads so that people spend their time and money to venture up here. The targeted audience obviously must be of the natural and organic bent. Why not capitalize on the obvious? Try this idea out: a panoramic background, with a bunch of healthy, suntanned hikers munching down on some local flora, with the announcer saying, "If you make the trip, the meal's on us."

Alaskans find themselves going out to gather nature's bounty not so much because of the idea that eating all sorts of wild vegetable matter is healthy, nor is it simply the lure of free grub. No, it's another one of those things we do because our license plates tell us we live in "The Last Frontier." It's an obligation we feel, to live up to the Alaskan mystique. The real, old-time Sourdoughs didn't rely on the local grocery. Fast food was whatever could be picked on the trail without breaking stride.

The list of what is edible in the Alaskan wilds is lengthy. However, the list of what is palatable is not. After several years of intensive study, I can personally assure you that there is a distinct and important difference between edible and palatable.

One of the first edible plants to lure the outdoor gourmet into shopping the woodlands is the fiddlehead fern. The snow is still receding when this delicacy first becomes available. The object of interest will be found in the center of a clump of rotting fern leaves left from the previous year. Once the site is located, close examination will reveal new leaves unfurling in the shape of fiddleheads. Those are what the reference books tell you taste "just like asparagus." You may have to poke around in the decaying slime of the old leaves to find them, but that only adds to the eager anticipation. Snap a bunch of those off, and make haste for the kitchen.

In all the references available, the first step listed in preparing fiddleheads is to remove the brown outer covering. Not a single hint on how to accomplish this task is given. The natural inclination is to grab a stiff bristled brush and scrub it off. This will produce a brilliant green mush laced with shreds of brown protective covering. Soaking the fiddleheads doesn't appreciably soften the casing either. Scraping the covering off gently with a knife produces the desired results, but tedium usually forces a quick, and less than complete job.

Once they are cleaned to your satisfaction and/or tedium tolerance level, the fiddleheads are placed in a pan and steamed for a few minutes. Again, the references don't provide any guide-lines. I believe the idea is to get them hot enough to melt butter, but not so cooked that they slither through the tines of a fork. The time frame between the two extremes is narrow, and it is a definite must to test the progress with a fork. But don't stir, or you'll end up with creamed green stuff.

When at last they are done, the whole family will be lined up with plates in hand. This glorious occasion is probably the first time in their young lives that the children have been excited about setting a tooth into a vegetable. The moment is electric. Mom will probably want to pull out the fine china, normally reserved for really special table fare. Just hope there's enough to go around.

The big moment arrives, and everyone is dished up and at the table. Mom and Dad are feeling good about truly providing. This is not just a meal mind you, but a genuinely *natural* and *totally organic* meal.

Dad glances around the table waiting for praise, "So, what d'ya think kids?"

"It's so... *green*. How'd you get it so *green*, Mom?"

"And it smells funny too, Dad. Like when I clean out the pencil sharpener at school."

Dad isn't about to be put off. "Nonsense! Put a little more butter on, that'll make it so you like it. See? Mom likes it. Don't you dear? Hon? You okay?"

The drift of attention is focused on Mom, whose face has puckered in on itself. She looks like a shar-pei that just bit a lemon as she jumps up and dashes to the garbage to discharge the offensive stuff.

Dad can't believe it. "I thought you liked asparagus."

"Not when it tastes like number two pencil shavings."

This is not a display fitting of true Alaskans. Dad knows that with a little leadership, the family will come around. He takes a bite. "Interesting..."

Pride will make a man do strange things. He tries to swallow. He tries again. The vegetable mass is growing. The kids stare in wide-eyed awe.

"Oh jeez, Mom! Lookit his Adam's apple! How's he makin' it jump around like that?"

Dad's as green as the fiddleheads left on his plate. With one mighty, forceful "*GURP*," Dad chokes it down. "So, I'm feelin' like a burger and fries. How about you guys?"

Fiddlehead ferns aren't the only item that may be edible but not palatable. There exists a veritable smorgasbord out on the Alaskan countryside, and other available delights deserve their space and time.

Herbal teas are a must for the natural food fan. What's the point in enjoying the wild gastronomic delights that will create a healthier you if they are washed down with something that is laden with sugar, chemicals or caffeine? In order to reap the full benefit of naturally organic food, the beverage of choice is an herbal tea.

The term herbal tea is somewhat ambiguous. The name would connote a delightful and delicate brew. An herbal tea should have some sort of beneficial effect. The current usage of the label "herbal" just guarantees that there's something in the hot water. Whether or not it is delicate, delightful, beneficial, or even just plain ambivalent to the drinker is of no consideration. Take spruce tip tea as an example.

One reference I read described this concoction, made from the new growth tips of spruce trees, as "aromatic and bright; an eye-opener." I'd agree with that assessment, but the same could be said for sipping on a boiling cup of turpentine. However, to give credit where it is due, spruce tip tea does have a beneficial effect when brewed after camping for three days without a toothbrush. Who needs clean and minty when one can have pine-fresh breath?

Rose hips provide as close a pleasant herbal tea as can be found. The flavor truly is palatable. The problem is that in order to obtain a full flavor, the rose hips must be steeped to just this side of disintegration. A few extra seconds of brewing time will yield a cup half full of mucilaginous rose hip remnants. Even the most enthusiastic herbal tea fanatic will balk at the thick end of rose hip tea.

Dried rose hips are also highly touted as a snack. Splitting and cleaning rose hips is a simple affair, requiring nothing more than the skill of a surgeon and the patience of a saint. The references recommend enjoying your dried rose hips as a garnish on cereal. Some go as far as to say that dried rose hips are equivalent to a crunchy treat, offering a "pleasant surprise." Sure. I'd bet whoever wrote that also loves finding those little rocks that surprise you now and then in corn chips.

Most books also suggest just munching on dried rose hips as a vitamin-C rich snack. The difficulty is they can absorb more saliva than the average human can produce in a lifetime, so have plenty of water nearby to wash them down. That's what prevents me from enjoying them. Not that they are dry, but the thought of what rose hips turn into when they get wet.

While there are many people who don't want to experience rose hips, almost everybody likes berries. At least they say they do. When two people swap notes on berries, the first question that comes up is usually, "What do *you* do with them?"

Obviously, the answer should be, "Oh, I just pop 'em in my mouth and enjoy."

That, however, is not the common answer. What is more likely to be heard is a recipe for pies, or jams and jellies. All those recipes could be paraphrased into the statement, "Oh, I just cook the bejabbers out of 'em and then add four cups of sugar to each cup of berries." Most folks don't know what just plain berries taste like anymore.

Of course, the names given to the berries don't help, either. The first year I decided to try foraging, I ran out and slurped down some of those yummy "watermelon berries." We're talking serious misnomer here.

The more honest name of moss berries, also called crow berries, doesn't generate any high hopes, and that is fortunate. However, I must admit that my favorite berry recipe is for moss berries. It is a typical cook beyond recognition, fill pot with sugar recipe, except the cook adds large amounts of orange peel and juice. The person that passed the recipe on to me wrote on the bottom of the card, "Tastes just like orange marmalade." I don't know if it does or not; I've never actually tried it. It's my favorite recipe simply because that last promise is so appealing.

Cranberries have a name that anyone who has ever celebrated Thanksgiving can associate with. The difference between our two strains and what is commercially grown is in tartness. Commercial cranberries are tart. Our wild cranberries will make a person pucker hard enough to choke on their own eyeballs.

Even weeds get into the act. Fireweed sprouts are cherished by some as a salad green. No claims of "tastes just like..." are made.

To me, they taste just like Ranch or Italian dressing, depending on what's in the house.

Once the fireweed blooms, the blossoms are also frequently used in salads for a kind of Great Land parsley effect. I won't eat the blossoms. I find the thought of eating something that flying insects were sticking their tongues into as I picked it, repugnant.

Let there be no doubt that Nature's gifts are a treat. I can't offer an argument against their health benefits, and yes, they are definitely free for the picking. But as most Alaskans have discovered, I've found the best way to enjoy them is by sharing them. Particularly with out-of-town guests, visiting relatives and other unsuspecting souls. Being there for the sharing is their greatest virtue. And who knows? Maybe I'll even discover somebody that actually likes them someday.

Warning Signs

Statistically speaking, Alaskans live in one of the most dangerous places in the country. With all the physically demanding and challenging activities at our doorsteps, coupled with living in an area that has inclement weather and rugged terrain, it isn't difficult to understand why.

I think most folks just accept the fact that some of their activities have a certain amount of risk involved. In fact, risk is the only attraction that some activities have going for them-- bungee jumping being a prime example. One young person I know told me, "Three out of five first time jumpers get so scared, they scream and lose bladder control. Isn't that rad?" Sounds like a prudent and sensible reason to spend the money to me. Anyone with a toddler can watch the same kind of action in the comfort of their own home. Thanks, but no thanks; I've done my time with potty training mishaps.

There are two very opposite ends to the risk spectrum: those that seek it out for enjoyment, and those that wish to wipe it out in any form that it may exist. For every crazed bungee jumper, you have a crazed danger elimination freak.

Bungee jumpers don't bother me nearly as much as their opposites. The people I'm talking about are those folks that are attempting to protect us from ourselves, the stick on a warning sign, rig it so it won't run, eliminate any kind of possible danger people. They are the thoughtful, well-meaning persons that have been compelled to remind us to stay back fifty feet from garbage trucks and snowplows, not to play in dumpsters, and always close the cover before striking matches. Had they stopped with just those basic instructions, there wouldn't be a problem.

Unfortunately, they have become vocal and pushy to the point that their desire to save us from ourselves is beginning to pervade every aspect of our lives.

For example, examine any new lawn mower. They are a far cry from the old Acme Turf-Trimmer used in my youth. I particularly like the sage advice about not sticking hands and feet under the deck while the blade is turning.

"Well, lookee here Martha! Says right here: 'DO NOT stick hands or feet under the mower when the blade is turning.' Shoot! They take all the fun outta chores."

I have personally known only one person that has been injured with a lawn mower. That fellow lost a portion of his big toe when he stepped on a doggy deposit while mowing down a hill, slipped, and his foot slid under the deck.

I feel confident in stating that gentleman did not give much forethought into putting his foot under the deck of that mower. Of course, I may be wrong, as this was in the time before warning stickers were mandated.

In order to stem the tide of countless accidents that occur yearly as people from coast to coast slip on dog-doo and slide under their mowers, the warning/danger people have deemed it necessary to go a step further than just providing every mower with a sticker that states the obvious. They have made sure every new mower sold today has an annoying "brake bar" that stops the mower when released. One either holds the bar down all the time, or the engine is killed and a brake applied to stop the blade from turning. This is a good idea, unless you want to: a) work on the engine, b) bend over to remove an object (that is obviously *not* under the deck), c) wash out the underside where all the grass is clinging, or d) just let the darn mower idle while you step away to say something about a cold drink to your spouse.

Any of those situations now require restarting the mower. Which, by the way, must be done by pulling the rope with only one hand, as the other hand is busy holding the stupid bar down. It has become a situation where a digit saved is a back thrown out.

Warning/danger people admonitions are not limited to mechanized items. I saw the newest warning/danger people fad just the other day. While looking for a new pair of scissors, I noticed a warning label on one pair that said, "Caution: sharp edges."

"Oh *no*, Fluffy, not sharp edges! Honey, I don't want to use this dangerous pair of scissors. Would you get me the ones with the round, soft edges?"

The warning found on toilet bowl cleaners always makes me chuckle. Right there, under the brazen claims of being able to strip away the most stubborn iron buildup, the grungiest soap scum accumulations and crusts of lime to be found, is the warning "Do not get in eyes." I cannot tell you how many times I have read such containers and thought, "Gee, I wonder what this would do to the soft and delicate tissues of my eyes?"

Over explanation seems to be the rule of thumb for warning/danger people. How else could one explain the signs stating, "Avalanche Area: Do Not Stop"? It is definitely a good thing to advertise the potential danger of avalanches in certain areas. There is no question about that, but the part about "Do Not Stop" is an insult to one's intelligence.

"Honey, what say we pack the kids up and picnic in the avalanche area?"

Some warning signs are simply pointless. How many times, when the equipment is in actual operation, is it possible to read the sign on the back of those huge snow plow trucks that say "Keep Back 100 Feet?" If the sign can be seen, let alone read, you are much closer than one hundred feet.

Not every single dangerous situation has been properly identified by these noble folk, at least not yet. Here is just a smattering of warnings yet to come:

- Do not lick beaters while mixer is in operation.
- Do not use Weed Whacker to trim mustache.
- Do not sit on wood stove while in use.
- Do not close door before walking through.
- Do not wear golf shoes while on waterbed.
- Do not test waffle iron with bare hand.
- Do not urinate on spark plug wire while engine is running.
- Do not store sharpened fish hooks in nasal passages.

- Do not stand directly under glacier while calving.
- Do not exit aircraft, while in flight, without first donning a parachute.
- Do not feed grizzlies with bare hands.

It's a scary, dangerous world out there. Maybe we ought to institute a universal warning sticker, something simple and easy to remember. Something along the line of, "Don't be stupid," would probably do the job, but be careful how you peel the backing off. There is the potential danger of a paper cut.

Tripped Outside

Most Alaskans have relatives "Outside." Even those few that can substantiate the claim that they were born and raised here will have someone that lives beyond our state lines that they call "kin."

This fact has a definite positive side. For example, if there is some occasion that requires a gift, there is no fear in sending one that will be a repeat. I would venture to say that no newly wed couple in Coon's Creek, Iowa has ever uttered the words, "Oh darn! Another ulu. We'll have to see if we can exchange it."

Equally unlikely is a Lower Forty-eight high school graduate that bemoans the fact that they have too many fluorescent scaled salmon ties or moose nugget earrings. And how many households in the Lower Forty-eight worry about which "Moosel-toe" to hang during the Yule season? Very few, if any, no doubt. The list is as endless as it is tasteless.

Another advantage to Outside relatives, is that one need not live in fear of Uncle Mort and Aunt Millie simply dropping by unannounced. Unexpected visits by relatives are generally not a problem with distances that exceed two thousand miles.

However, living here does not guarantee a totally Utopian existence when it comes to dealing with physically distant relatives. Sooner or later, the time arrives when "the big trip down south" becomes unavoidable. It is only a matter of time before some relative corners you into a conversation that will allow no escape except to agree upon a visit.

Visiting itself isn't a hardship. It's everything that leads up to, and the events that transpire during the visit that are hardships.

Much planning and preparation goes into a southbound safari. It isn't something that is decided upon as a pleasant diversion for a rainy Saturday. No, trips to see relatives south of the Canadian border are an endeavor guaranteed to tax the most logistically gifted.

The Alaskan traveler is at the mercy of the airlines. It doesn't matter when you plan on traveling, seat availability will be low, and prices will be high. I have to confess that I don't understand the airlines' logic. At the height of tourist season, prices are high because, well, it's tourist season. In the dead of winter, prices are high because, well, it's the off season.

Another problem associated with flying is that there are no direct flights that either begin or terminate during normal waking hours. It's as if the airlines are determined to amplify any "jet-lag" by starting or ending your trip at a bizarre hour.

"Hello, you've reached Bye-bye Travel and Septic Systems, how may I help you?"

"Yes, I'd like to make reservations to fly to San Francisco in two months from tomorrow, the twentieth. Four will be going."

"Ah yes, just a moment." There is a great deal of clicking on a keyboard, and the travel agent returns, "We have the two A.M. flight or the nine-thirty P.M. flight. How many in your party, four? Oh no, I'm wrong. The evening flight is full except for first-class."

"Ahem, do you have any day flights?"

"Not direct," more keyboard play, "we do have a flight that leaves at nine A.M. for Salt Lake. Arrival at five-fifty P.M. That will connect with a flight to Phoenix at eight-fifteen. On to Los Angeles at nine-fifty-five. Then to San Francisco, arriving at one-twenty A.M."

Air transportation isn't the least of the worries. Upon the eventual arrival at the final destination, ground transportation will be needed.

All travel agents ask, "Shall I reserve a car?" They do this with an air of competence that would lead one to believe that there will actually be a vehicle at your disposal upon arrival. The agents even go so far as to claim knowledge of what type of vehicle might be available. "Los Alamos has a special on their economy cars. You can qualify for the 'I love Yugo' special by reserving now. You'll get a luxurious, new Yugo with air conditioning, and unlimited mileage for only $24.50 a day. This, of course, doesn't include tax, insurance, fuel charge, surcharge, deposit or cleaning fee."

In actual fact, the traveler's choices are simple: walk, take an upgrade upon arrival, or just reserve the ultra-luxury car to begin with.

With itinerary in hand, it's time to call the relatives and announce the big plans.

Relatives are kind. They know the arduous task of making all the travel arrangements has probably left you exhausted. Being so kind, they will have, no doubt, taken it upon themselves to plan how you will spend every last minute of your time visiting.

"It's all set. We'll get there early Saturday."

"Oh, good. Kathy, Mike and the kids will be down in the afternoon. Then Sunday Dad has you, Mike, Uncle Bert and himself signed up for the Elk's Golf Tourney. Monday we'll all go shop-ping. Tuesday we'll drive down and see Aunt Myrtle for a couple of days..."

Every Alaskan visitor has at least one set of not quite distant enough relatives. Those are the relatives that live just within semi-reasonable driving distance. Typically, the relationship with these relatives isn't close enough to warrant communication, other than Christmas cards. However, the relationship is close enough for them to be highly offended if the additional two hundred mile drive to see them isn't made. They could always drive to where you are, but know that "you'll probably be ready to see a little of the countryside." Besides, after several thousand miles of travel, what's a little drive? Right? And don't forget the unlimited mileage on the rental. You owe it to yourself to get your money's worth.

All of this is enough to force the question, "Why do we put ourselves through this?"

Why? Because they're family. Because when you get there, and the whole motley group pours out the door, and the little kids dance up and down in excitement, and hugs get passed around, and all the faces beam with pleasure at your safe arrival, you'll hear those three words that you can always count on family to say: "Where's the salmon?"

Snow Removal

There is nothing that builds up over the winter, and weighs as heavily on the mind during break-up, than the thought of snow removal. March and early April in Alaska exist for deep reflections on the entire snow removal season. It's just like the post-season evaluation of an NCAA basketball team's performance.

"Well Coach, how would you evaluate your team's performance this year? Any regrets? Any changes for next year?"

"Well Marv, I'll tell ya. We started out strong. First few weeks of the season we showed a lot of hustle, good movement, a lot of mobility. Late season wasn't so great; things just kind of got piled up on us. We shoulda gone high early in the season; the roof's a mess. We don't look good on the ground either, we're at the bottom of the heap. We're gonna look at new strategy for next season, and maybe make a couple of new acquisitions."

Fortunately, just like a sports team, Alaskans can evaluate their performance in snow removal and make adjustments for the next season. Unfortunately, they have to.

The perfect snow removal season is like the perfect sports season: an anomaly, a fluke. There is no way to take into account all the variables. There are however, a few basics that will help ease the novice through the first couple of winters with only minimal damage to home and health.

What is the first thing that everyone runs out and buys the first year? That's right, a snow shovel. That's where the first mistake is made. A full *set* of snow shovels is needed. Many people buy just one shovel their first fall. How long does it last? Until the second good dump of snow. After that, it isn't seen again until everything melts.

Not only is it necessary to keep a good number of shovels on hand, but several different styles should be kept available. You can't scoop snow with a push style blade, and you can't shove slush with a big, flat blade. A shovel with a long, straight handle is good for pushing snow down slopes, a short handle with a grip is best for pitching. Shovels with bent, ergonomic handles are good for nothing except to serve as loaners to people you never want to borrow anything from you again, so at least three of those are needed.

Steel blades hold up the best, aluminum is lightweight for those big jobs, and plastic is worthless for anything but to serve as a decoy to fool would-be borrowers. Oddly enough, the shovels with ergonomic handles come with plastic blades. (Maybe six is a better number to keep in stock.)

Only those hardy souls that enjoy frigid aerobics, or have very short driveways, are long satisfied with manual snow removal. Most folks move up into high-tech snow removal after their first herniated disk. Snow blowers are the first step into high-tech snow removal.

There exist numerous kinds of snow blowers, but they are basically broken down into two categories: those that cause the operator mere physical discomfort, and those that cause actual physical harm. Of the latter group, those little electrically powered scoops that cut a twelve inch swathe by flinging the snow straight into the air are the most dangerous.

My neighbor, Blizzard Bob, had one of those, which is how he got his name. One day, he became disoriented in the snow blower produced ground blizzard, wandered off his driveway, and buried himself. Had I not gone over to borrow a snow shovel, and noticed the extension cord dangling out of a large snow drift, he might have come to an ill end. After we dug him free of the drift and thawed him out, he immediately got rid of the electric scoop and moved up to the next step in snow removal.

38

The next step up in the mechanical snow removal line is the gas powered snow blower with genuine rubber paddled auger. These babies can, with a good stiff wind, almost throw the snow all the way off a narrow sidewalk. They work (or don't, depending on whether you're actually using one, or just reading the brochure), on the principal of a compressed volume of snow following the path of least resistance. New owners quickly discover that the path of least resistance is generally back out in front of the auger. The worst models of this type run for years. The best models fall apart rapidly, affording the owner the opportunity to buy a two- stage snow blower.

Once a person gets serious about snow removal, the two-stage snow blower becomes a necessity. These contraptions, powered by a gas engine of five horsepower or better, are all heavy steel construction. They all have huge, spiral shaped initial augers, located in the scoop, that grind and force snow, ice, and small import cars into the second stage.

The second stage consists of rapidly spinning paddles that throw the compressed snow out the chute for considerable distances. The chute can be rotated to throw the snow stream in any direction, which generally happens to be into the prevailing wind.

Since two-stage snow blowers are so large, they are self-propelled. The drive systems have several speed selections, ranging from "back-over-operator" to "drag-operator." Once moving, there is little that can stop a two-stage snow blower, except a mislaid newspaper. Newspapers are the Achilles' heel of the two-stage snow blower. A newspaper sucked into the scoop stops the main auger, causing the belts that turn it to disintegrate. The resultant screeching goes on long after the snow blower is turned off. I love to sneak up on Blizzard Bob, who has graduated to the two-stage snow blower now, and shout, "Weekly supplement!"

It generally only takes about three or four seasons to force the homeowner up to the next step of high-tech snow removal: push button removal. This is such a simple method some folks cheat themselves out of years of stimulating excitement by resorting to it immediately. Push button snow removal is accomplished by picking up your phone and pushing the buttons to call a professional with a plow. Nothing could be easier. There is no sweat involved, no personal physical hazards, no challenge, and no way it could really be that carefree.

The biggest problem involved with push button snow removal is finding the right buttons to push. Your neighbor down the street is going to protect his snow plower's number like it was the combination to his safe. Lots of mean spirited pranksters post phony snow plowing ads on the bulletin boards at the local malls. These deceptive ads can be identified by the use of certain words and phrases.

The word "cheap" is the first that comes to mind, but the word "cheap" is subjective, so it could be found in a legitimate ad. A dead give away for one of the phony ads is the phrase "quick service." Snow removal specialists are professionals, just like a doctor. Hence, you *will* be kept waiting.

The only true method for identifying a phony snow removal ad is to call the number. A response of, "Oh, I dunno... I might be able to squeeze you in, oh... say a week from tomorrow maybe..." is the sure sign of a valid number.

Push button removal takes error production out of the homeowner's control, and lays it firmly on the shoulders of the professional. A good snow removal professional reduces the homeowner's responsibility to strictly deciding where the snow should be piled. With their large, powerful trucks, equipped with wide, stout blades, these people are paid to give you peace of mind, and the option of where to put the new water well in the spring.

Regardless of the removal system used, either high-tech or manual, the big problem remains: where to put all the snow? This is no easy task. No matter how far snow is thrown or shoved, either by hand or mechanically, it isn't far enough. Those mounds of snow will turn into streams of water in April. This is where the real evaluation of the season takes place. This is what separates the experienced snow removers from the neophytes. Those experienced in snow removal have their sandbags piled and ready by the doors.

Winter Camping With Kids

Real camping (using tents, sleeping bags, and the hard, cold ground as opposed to a motorhome) is a pastime that has a certain amount of peril to it. Think about it. There is a definite reason as to why the "mountain men" of long ago had a life expectancy of roughly 36 years: real camping as a lifestyle will kill you. The occasional real camper can attest to the wear and tear on the body.

Real camping with kids is even more perilous because of the inherent possibility that your mind will be at least as damaged as your body. Kids add an "edge" to camping. The adult's job when camping with kids is not to step off the edge.

There are a few basic rules that go along when real camping with kids. The first is: the adults will not get any sleep. This is because someone must stay awake to tell the kids to go to sleep. Since kids forget where the outhouse is as soon as the sun goes down, the adult is also obligated to serve as the outhouse trip traffic coordinator.

"Go to sleep, son."

"I gotta go to the outhouse."

"Again? You just went ten minutes ago!"

"I couldn't find it, but I found a totally awesome, dried up, dead fish head. Got it in my sleeping bag. Here."

Another tenet when real camping with kids is that the firewood supply is never enough for a "good" fire. It doesn't matter that an entire cord of firewood occupied the back of the truck. To kids, the wood supply will always be at least one stick short of a satisfactory fire.

"Whoa, dude! Lookit the side of the cooler. It's like, melting."

"Oh, way rad, man! If we only had like, just one more stick of wood, we could make Dad's waders smoke."

Normally, at this point, having collapsed in exhaustion from unloading and stacking the firewood, the adult wakes up screaming. With both feet boiling in their own perspiration, the adult launches into the traditional camping with kids clog dance: *hop-hop, grab boot, burn hand, hop-hop, grab boot, burn hand.*

The final given when real camping with kids is that in the valiant effort to stave off total starvation, at least one of the little campers will eat until they get sick. The intensity of the illness is directly proportional to how hungry the kid was just prior to dinner.

Real camping in winter is even tougher. It requires conditioning and self-control. One must be in a condition of total mental degeneration, and use tremendous amounts of self- control to keep from whining loud enough to draw predators into camp.

Real camping with kids in winter is, well, stupid. However, since so much of the year in Alaska has what would be considered ideal winter camping conditions, it is inevitable that the average camping family will spend time in the winter camping mode.

All of the usual summer rules apply when real camping with kids in the winter, plus a few more.

Real camping with kids in winter additional rule number one: the three-person tent is a myth. Any three-person tent in the summer is a tight fit at the rated capacity. In the winter, with the addition of gear, bulkier sleeping bags, and extra clothing, fitting three people into a three person tent is an impossibility unless everyone wants to give up breathing. Even then, it's a close call.

After everyone has crowded into the tent, additional rule number two begins: kids expel five times their body weight in moisture when in a winter tent. This is not just a simple rule, this is an amazing natural phenomenon that can produce a six inch snowfall *inside* the tent over the course of one night. Many adults have awakened screaming *"Avalanche!"* after someone has carelessly bumped the side of the tent.

Amazing additional rule number three: there is not a sleeping bag in use by anyone under the age of eighteen that has a zipper that will stay up. This rule has a corollary: if a zipper does manage to stay up, it's because it is stuck, and will be on the sleeping bag that contains the kid who ate four bowls of chili, three bags of chips, a couple dozen cookies, while washing it all down with at least a gallon of cherry Kool-Aid, and who is now sick.

The basic camping with kids firewood rule applies to winter camping with kids. Additionally, there is the winter rule of campfire zones. A winter campfire with kids has two zones: the outer zone which, at its warmest edge, contains no detectable heat, and the inner zone which, at its coldest edge, is just under the ignition point of most leather and rubber boots. This rule results in the paradoxical situation in which campfires cause cold feet.

"Awesome, man! Lookit the way the snow sticks to your boots when you walk away from the fire."

"Rad."

"Yeah. Now go back to the fire and do it again."

"Oh, gnarly! You can make your feet into like, ice blocks, dude."

The duties assumed by the adult serving as the night shift outhouse trip traffic coordinator have two of their own special winter rules. The first is: no kid will need to make a trip to the outhouse until the adult is zipped up, snug and warm, in their sleeping bag.

"Settle down. *Now!!*"

"I gotta go. Can I just, you know, like go outside the tent real fast?"

"No way, kiddo. Hoof it all the way to the outhouse."

"It's dark out there. Where's the flashlight?"

This brings us to special rule number two for the winter time night shift outhouse trip traffic coordinator: no flashlight battery will have any power after the sun sets.

"Here's the flashlight, see ya when you get back."

"It's not working. Look."

Sure enough, any light shed from the bulb is not detectable over the brilliance of your luminescent watch dial.

"Okay, I'll go with you."

"I don't understand it, Dad. It worked all those times I tested it earlier today."

There is one, final rule to winter camping with kids: the rule of incubation. The rule of incubation dictates that all serious infections in an adult will only incubate, and not manifest any symptoms, until the adult has set up camp and managed get the young campers to

43

settle down. Then, in the middle of a sub-zero night, miles from the nearest bottle of aspirin, a raging fever, chills, double pneumonia and sinus infection will strike.

The worst part about this rule is that the illness, although agonizing, will rarely prove fatal. There will be more winter camping in the future.

Winter Sports

When the first snow has fallen, the season of winter sports commences. We are not talking about Olympic competition here. These sports are just something to make life in Alaska a little more fun and interesting.

Winter sports have some distinct advantages: there are no initial sign-up fees, there is no need to make court reservations, they can be played alone or in groups, and most are covered by insurance of one sort or another.

There are also some minor disadvantages to winter sports: you never know when you're going to play, you generally can't choose your partners, and joining in on the fun might cause insurance cancellation.

One need not necessarily be an athlete of any sort in order to be one of the top competitors. Style, not prowess, is what counts. This is especially true of the first, and most common winter sport, "slip, boogie and flop," which is played on any available flat, icy surface.

The object in this competition is to change from an upright, normal walking gait to a horizontal position on the ground after completing a series of freestyle acrobatic gyrations while running in place at full speed. As in bronc riding, extra points can be earned by keeping one arm in motion and raising the knees high. If performed properly, a crowd of spectators will gather around to admire the final position. Extra points are awarded for groups larger than five persons that show concern over the player's well-being (ambulance attendants do not count). Points are lost for each minute taken to return to an upright, standing position, or if assistance is needed to recover. A player will default their attempt if the word "lawsuit" or any derivative thereof is uttered.

The "mukluk sock slough" is a little more passive. In this sport, the object is to completely remove one's socks without removing one's boots or mukluks first. The rules are simple. By walking only in a normal fashion, a sock no less than mid-calf in length must be stuffed into the toe of the player's boot or mukluk. Upon removal of the boot or mukluk, no portion of the foot is to be covered by the sock. Points are deducted for socks that do not have any elastic in them, for footwear sizes larger than the player's normal shoe size, and for attempts that take longer than fifteen minutes.

In testing a person's perseverance and stamina in dealing with sub-zero temperatures, the "mitten manipulation" event has no equal. This sport is reserved for those periods of time when the ambient temperature has dropped to levels where any normal outside activity is all but impossible due to the necessary layers of clothing. The required equipment is a set of keys and a pair of thick mittens.

Play begins as the competitor stands out in the cold, trying to manipulate the key needed to open a car or home while wearing mittens. Points are earned for each minute the player stands out in the cold, refusing to remove the mittens. The event is completed when the player finally gets disgusted, pulls off the mittens and freezes their fingers to the cryogenic keys. One extra point is earned for each time the key ring is dropped and retrieved with the mittens, and points are doubled if the keys are dropped in snow over ten inches deep. One extra point is also added for wind-chill, based upon each five mile per hour increase over dead calm.

Later in the winter sports season, many people have the opportunity to compete in "the slide for life." This sport combines the grace and agility of "slip, boogie and flop" with the derring-do of bungee jumping. Starting in a position at the peak of the competitor's roof (generally somewhere near the TV antenna), the player starts out in a fashion similar to "slip, boogie and flop," proceeds to the flat position on the roof, and then goes on to what is best described as a sort of running break dance routine while sliding toward the edge of the roof.

This is a complicated event to score. Points are earned on the basis of distance traveled in the flat position, how deeply the fingernails gouge into the roofing material, and how close to the roof's edge the player stops. Extra points are awarded to screams that are above "high C," screams that last longer than ten seconds, stops that leave more than just the feet dangling from the eaves, and perfect snow angels that are made upon impact should a stop not be achieved. Points are lost for extreme profanity, and/or whimpering after impact.

One of the few competitions that involves team competition is the "uphill push." This sport is a three person event, involving one driver and two coaches.

The game starts when the driver stops (either on their own accord or from external forces such as poorly placed ditches etc.) at the bottom of a hill, and then ascertains that resuming any forward motion is impossible without the aid of a push. Two coaches are selected from passengers, innocent passersby, or any combination thereof. The coaches are then positioned directly behind each rear wheel of the vehicle. The action starts when a mutually agreed upon signal is given, and the driver tries to punch the vehicle's accelerator through the floorboard while rocking back and forth in the seat. The coaches shout encouragement and give continual updates on the progress not being made, as they lean against the rear of the vehicle and run in place.

The object of the sport is to reduce the coaches to sweaty, gasping imitations of snowmen while failing to make any detectable forward progress. Extra points are given for spinning the tires right into the dirt and pelting the coaches with gravel, or managing to fishtail completely off the road.

Another great vehicular winter sport is the "high speed coffee clutch berm jump." This event most often takes place in the early morning hours following a little preparation by the nightshift of the municipal, borough or state snow relocation crews.

The event begins as the player gets into their vehicle with one last steaming cup of java for the trip to work. As the end of the driveway nears, the player responds to the visible snow berm by accelerating to ramming speed while holding the coffee cup high in the air. The object of the event is to achieve break-through with as much of the coffee still in the cup as possible.

A point is earned for each ounce of coffee that remains in the cup. An extra point is given for shifting manual transmissions, and/or trying to sip the blistering coffee during impact. Points are deducted for the use of four wheel drive, getting high centered, and each ounce of coffee worn after impact.

Of course, this has just been a brief overview of the many possible winter sports that can brighten our days. Time and space limitations prevent a more thorough discussion of others such as the longjohn jitterbug, the one galosh gallop, the flaming oil pan bake, and the ever popular frozen pipe tongue touch.

It's funny, but I almost feel sorry for those poor folks stuck in Hawaii. With just one sunny tropical day after another, they don't know the fun they're missing.

More Moosecapades

Having a moose mistake your yard for a bed and breakfast during the frigid and unforgiving months of winter is bad news. They are cranky and obstinately refuse to leave, taking great offense at even the most gentle of hints to move on. Fortunately, such visitations are normally short-lived, with the moose seeking a new haunt within a day. It could be much worse: the moose could take up permanent residence.

One of my neighbors, Blizzard Bob (or B.B., as he is more commonly referred to), relocates as much snow as he can during the winter months. The snow relocation goes beyond need, it is a compulsion. B.B. will be out with his turbo-charged Belch-Flame Spewmaster snow thrower whenever he can. Not satisfied with simply removing the snow from his driveway, Bob likes to maintain a meticulous path that loops around the side of his house. He also clears off his back deck. All this not only makes for easy access to his wood pile, but it also creates the perfect protected area that must look like a welcoming moose hostel.

One evening, when B.B. stepped out the back door to grab some firewood, he encountered one of the neighborhood's resident moose. He didn't even see the large, ancient cow until she jumped up and whirled to face him with lowered head. From that point on, whatever the cow did is pure speculation, as B.B. was preoccupied with trying to claw his way back through the door.

He claims she snorted and then clipped him with a hoof. The affair could probably be described as a high adrenaline situation. B.B. declined to display the bruise, stating that we'd all just have to take his word for it as he was determined to preserve one small shred of dignity.

With the back porch staunchly guarded, B.B. was forced to walk around his house from the front, and carefully pick up his wood supply. With the moose located just four or five cords away, this job was accomplished rather gingerly.

The next night, B.B. was more circumspect in his approach to bringing in the firewood. He carefully cracked the back door and peered out. There was the moose, bedded down, right in the middle of the porch. The firewood was again carried in the long way.

On the third night, the moose was again bedded down on the porch. B.B. was tired of toting his firewood the long way around. He carefully opened the door and shouted at the cow, then quickly ducked back inside. After waiting a few minutes, he looked out the door again. The cow hadn't even bothered to move. Obviously, this was one tough customer. It was time to call for reinforcements. Knucks Mahoneigh, B.B.'s hunting and fishing partner was the logical choice. Besides respecting Knucks for his woodsman abilities and incredible knowledge of animal lore, he lives right next door.

"Hey, Knucks, I need your help. You got any of that Moose-be-gone stuff?"

"What? You mean that pepper spray bear repellent? Yeah, I've got a can in my pack, somewhere... I think."

"See if you can find it, and come on over."

After a few minutes of intense rummaging, the can of repellent was located, and Knucks headed over to Bob's. This wasn't so much an act of friendship as an act of curiosity. Knucks had always wondered if the spray would actually work. He'd heard unsettling rumors that sometimes the cans didn't actually spray. Here was an opportunity to try it out on something that, in all probability, wouldn't kill him, and definitely wouldn't eat him.

Upon arrival at Bob's, the plan of attack was explained. Knucks would lead the charge out the back door. Blizzard Bob would follow, screaming loudly. This would startle the moose and get her to jump up, thus offering a perfect target.

"Why do I have to lead the charge?"

"It's your spray. You can see if it works. I've heard sometimes the can doesn't spray."

"So? It's your moose. You should have the honors."

The debate continued for quite some time, but Bob finally won out with the logic that he knew precisely where the doorknob was in the off chance that things went awry.

They crouched by the door, ready to make the big assault. Knucks pulled the pin on the can, and nodded. Bob threw open the door and both of them jumped out onto the porch. Bob started yelling as they were mid-stride. Knucks mashed the trigger on the can the instant he landed on the patch of ice that threw his feet right out from under him. As he fell backwards, the trajectory of the spray arced up and back. B.B.'s yelling changed to a screaming pitch that would bring a look of envy from the Vienna Boy's Choir. As the spray settled, Knuck's voice joined in harmony.

Suddenly, Knucks felt a crushing blow to his chest. The cow was on him! He struck back, kicking and flailing wildly, screaming all the while.

Next, the cow got Bob. His yodeling was interrupted with guttural grunts from the impact of blows.

Knucks kicked harder and kept screaming, landing an occasional blow. Finally, he rolled, kicking and thrashing, as far as he could, and pressed himself against the packed snow surrounding Bob's porch.

The moose had stopped pounding Bob. He was somewhere on the other side of the porch, gasping.

After a few minutes, the intense burning in their eyes began to subside, and they could start to make things out. One of the first things they both saw was the moose. She was curled up right in the middle of the porch.

As they sat there transfixed, Knucks noticed something funny. "That old moose ain't breathing."

He crawled over to the cow and touched it, gently at first, then he slapped it hard. "That moose is deader than a stone, and froze solid to boot! I'll bet it's been dead two days or more. What'n hell were we fighting?"

B.B. got up and hobbled over to look for himself. After making a complete inspection, he sat down heavily on the frozen critter.

51

"Humph! Well I'll be! Hey, Knucks? Sorry I jumped on you after you fell down."

"Well, since this moose hasn't been what you'd call real active for the last two days, I'd say we're probably even. Whatcha going to do?"

Blizzard Bob looked at the large animal. Thoughts of what might lay ahead during the warmth of spring made him shudder. "Well, she's not a roadkill. Died of old age. Can't get in here with the truck to haul her off. Guess I'll have to cut her up."

"With what?"

"Chainsaw."

"Oh, man! That's rough on a chainsaw."

"Shouldn't be too bad if the chain's real sharp. Umm... Knucks, my chainsaw's broken. Can I borrow yours?"

B.B. would have never asked the question if he'd noticed Knucks was still holding the pepper spray.

Ice Fishing: a Hole Lotta Fun

In the winter, after the holidays are behind us, there is little to look forward to except the great, white expanse that yawns between us and break up. With cabin fever running rampant in homes, any sort of outside fun that breaks the inactivity starts to sound good. This period of time is especially hard on those of us that like to fish. We go nuts. In fact, we go nuts enough to get involved in an outside activity that consists mainly of standing in the middle of a frozen lake while staring into a hole in the ice.

Ice fishing is another one of those things most of us do simply because we are Alaskans. I know scores of people that like to fish, and never, not once, can I remember one of them saying in July, "Oh man! I can hardly wait 'till the lakes freeze over. This salmon fishing is okay, but you're not having fun unless your feet are cold."

In the course of human history, there were probably valid reasons for ice fishing; survival being the primary. What could have possibly kept this practice alive?

The pursuit of making this sport more pleasant has spawned numerous improvements on existing equipment, and has additionally been responsible for the invention of new items. Two notable examples are the power auger, which reduces arm strain and places it firmly on the fisherman's back, and the snowmobile which allows the fisherman to lug the power auger around. Of course, the advent of the snowmobile sled led to the folding ice fishing shanty, which brought about the catalytic heater, which in turn brought about the... well, the list is almost endless, and continually feeds itself.

So, what really is the purpose of ice fishing, beyond the collection of all sorts of neat doo-dads? Obviously, when one goes fishing in the summer, in the open water, there is the thrill of seeing the fish as it is played. There is little that matches the exhilaration felt when a big fish goes into a series of acrobatic maneuvers, jumping and splashing about. What does one get when ice fishing? Is it the incredible excitement of when the fish tries to jump, and thumps into the ice? "Oh, man! That was fantastic! That monster took off like a shot and ran... somewhere, I dunno where. Then it slammed into the ice three, maybe four times. Packed the snow down a good six inches. Is this great, or what?"

Is the purpose of ice fishing to provide spiritual renewal and fellowship? One would almost think so. People who ice fish lend credence to the old saying about misery loving company. Whenever the ice fishing is particularly productive, that is to say, whenever someone actually catches one fish over six inches, that particular spot gets a lot of attention. On a good day, a productive spot looks like some sort of religious ceremony is taking place. There are dozens of people standing around, staring at holes in the ice, while they sway to and fro, gently stomping their feet, chanting a mantra, "Ohhh fish, hummmm, ohhh fish."

That's all well and good, but still, none of the above are good *reasons* to go ice fishing. A moderately good reason for ice fishing is to get some exercise, and generally the only exercise equipment available following Christmas are ice augers. However, the auger itself only provides a small portion of the exercise. Once the hole drilling has the fisherman hot and sweaty, the real exercise begins: violent shivering.

The very best reason for going ice fishing is to fill up idle time. Too much idle time serves as fertile ground for the growth of boredom and the seeds of cabin fever. A long New Year's weekend presents itself as a virtual ripened manure pile, offering nutrient rich growth media for the immediate germination of boredom. Boredom being the direct result of endless college football "bowl" games.

This problem came up at a meeting of the NORSMen a few years ago. (NORSMen stands for North Road Supportive Men. It is a support group and an exclusive and benevolent society dedicated to the appreciation of cheap beer, bad cigars and good lies. The membership consists of Knucks Mahoneigh, B.B. and myself.) It was generally agreed that there is only so much "best team in the XXX Conference versus the best team in the YYY Conference" football one can tolerate. We ultimately decided that what was truly needed to spice things up was a "Toilet Bowl," where the two crappiest teams in America could compete for the singular honor of being the most statistically inferior organization in the sport. In lieu of such a bowl, it was decided that ice fishing could serve as a suitable alternative, and we would initiate the event and title it the "Fish Bowl."

While preparing for the first annual Fish Bowl, Knucks and I mentioned that we didn't own a functional auger. B.B. came to the rescue with a confident, "Don't worry, I've got it covered."

Upon arriving at the lake, the supplies for the adventure were loaded onto a plastic sled for easy transport. Knucks noticed there was no auger.

"Hey B.B., I thought you said you'd bring an auger. We can't fish without a hole."

"I never said I had an auger. I said I had it covered. I brought a spud; just as good as an auger." B.B. held up a long, solid metal pole with a thick, blunt wedge welded to one end.

The snow was cleared at a promising site, and B.B. put his spud into action. More snow was cleared away as the diameter of the hole grew to allow for the "most efficient spudding angle." Progress was slow: down a few inches, out a foot or more. The snow removal and spudding continued until the hole had grown to resemble a glacial strip mining operation.

Just as B.B. was almost played out, water began to seep into the bottom of the hole. He attacked the project with renewed zeal. He lifted the spud high, gave a mighty grunt, and jammed it down with all his might. The spud shattered through the thin ice at the bottom of the hole, slipped through B.B.'s weakened grip, and shot to the bottom of the lake. This left a two inch by two inch opening at the bottom of the crater for fishing. So much for the first annual Fish Bowl.

The second Fish Bowl found the NORSMen better prepared. B.B. made arrangements to borrow a power auger from a commercial fisherman friend of his. While loading the power auger onto the sled at the lake, we noticed the motor was well used, showing signs of considerable wear, while the auger blade was brand new, without a scratch to mar the painted surface.

"Wow. Your buddy must be an ice fishing fanatic," Knucks commented, "he's worn out an auger blade completely."

"Not at all," B.B. explained, "He's never even taken it ice fishing. That's the original blade. He uses the motor to turn his reel when he works on his nets in the off season. That's why the motor is so beat up. When I picked it up, he mentioned something about the connector being bent a little from the use, so we put the blade on it to make sure it still fit. Fits fine, but there's a little bit of an angle. It ought to do the job though."

We wandered out to a spot that looked promising and B.B. proceeded to set up the auger. A single pull on the starter rope was all it took to get the auger in action. There was most definitely a kink in the drive system: the top of the auger started whipping around as the blade bit into the ice. With a little trial and error, B.B. found that by hanging on tight and doing a little hula dance, he could pretty much keep the blade in one spot.

As the blade disappeared into the ice, B.B.'s hula shifted gears into a shimmy. Suddenly, the blade broke through the ice, snatching B.B. right down on top of the auger. B.B. slapped his face against the motor hard enough to split his lip and break a tooth. The second annual Fish Bowl was cut short with a third of the team sidelined with injuries.

The third annual Fish Bowl got off to an excellent start. We all chipped in a few dollars and bought a new hand auger.

Three holes were drilled without losing the auger, or causing any physical harm to the participants. After just a few minutes of fishing, we had each hooked a couple of small trout. It was all too perfect.

"Hey!" B.B. said as he stared intently at his hole, "I've got another one playing with my line."

"Me too," Knucks replied. "Betcha five bucks mine's bigger."

B.B. set his hook and shot back, "You're on."

Knucks' lightweight pole bent down sharply half a second after B.B. set the hook on his fish, and the contest was on.

It was obvious that both of the fishermen had something much bigger than what had been previously caught. Both men were cranking and hauling, reels singing as they gave up line to the big fish. B.B. would crank in, and Knucks would lose line. Knucks would heel back, and B.B.'s reel would scream.

B.B. was the first to notice a pattern to the fight. "Hey! I think we've got the same fish... every time I pull... *Omigosh!* It's *huge*! Knucks, cut your line so I can pull it in. It's enormous; gotta be at least five pounds!"

"Cut my line? Are you daft? Cut your own line."

"No, really: cut your line. I hooked it first, so it's really my fish."

I had to side with B.B., as his was the first strike.

Knucks was not pleased. "All right, but the bet is off."

"No problem... just *cut your line!*"

Knucks cut his line, and a few moments later B.B. pulled the fish through his hole. It was a tight fit. The fish was, indeed, magnificent. Unfortunately, it was a magnificent fish sporting only one hook.

Subsequent Fish Bowls have been canceled.

Christmas Lights

I find myself muttering those jolly holiday tunes over and over during the Christmas season. Not because I enjoy the songs so much, but because I find myself in need of a constant reminder to remain jolly.

Please don't get the impression that I humbug my way through the holidays. I truly enjoy sharing the spirit of Christmas with every person I meet during the hustle and crunch of shopping. Even the over saturation of Christmas carols droning on endlessly from all the radio stations doesn't put a pall on the situation.

No, that part of what should be a generally happy and pleasant season which has me mumbling a series of emphatic jollies is the annual stringing of Blizzard Bob's thermo-nuclear Yuletide display and the attendant power problems associated with it.

I'm not talking a mere sprinkling of luminarios or a cheerful display of a plastic Santa, but a full-blown, mega-wattage colossus of electrical engineering and duct tape. I'm talking Blizzard Bob's annual gift to the neighborhood and the Homer Electric Association.

This yearly production-- it goes on far too long, and is much too big to be simply described as a display-- began a few years ago when there was less snowfall than usual. Without the need to crank up his Belchflame Turbo-charged Spewmaster snowthrower, Blizzard Bob found himself with an excess of time and energy to while away after working on his coffee blends. The original idea was along the line of the Twelve Days of Christmas, with Bob setting out a new set of lights each night until his front yard was fairly ablaze with festivity on Christmas Eve.

Unfortunately, a few of us made the mistake of commenting on how much we enjoyed the show, and Bob has now become obsessed with making the display bigger and better each year by adding something new and more intricate. Now, construction begins in mid-November, and by mid-December Bob's electrical meter is spinning faster than a blender set to puree. Our end of the road suffers a brownout when the production is at its zenith. We have all learned to time our use of sensitive electrical appliances, such as computers, so that they are off when Bob fires up.

As the production grows, and the intensity of the light increases, so does the potential shock when the switch is thrown. A couple of years back, a moose was in the yard when Bob threw the switch. The poor critter was so dumbfounded that it stood frozen in its tracks for the entire night. As it had been munching on the hay Bob put out as part of the Nativity scene, the moose made a passable, albeit somewhat large, donkey. It is the general consensus in the neighborhood that the moose was the best display Bob has ever had.

The moose incident raised some concerns, however. With Blizzard Bob's lot being near an intersection, it was brought up that the initial flash might create a hazardous driving situation. We all felt that if a driver was caught unawares, the initial panic from the mistaken impression that there had been a nuclear attack might result in an accident.

A group of us went to Bob with this concern. His response was to fashion what looks like a large Christmas package out of painted plywood, with twinkling lights presenting the warning, "CAUTION: intense, blinding flashes possible. Have a Merry Christmas." So far, the warning has worked, but the UPS drivers won't deliver anything after dusk.

Ice fog has also caused problems. With most of the displays out and lit, the pulsating glare from all the bulbs in the ice fog creates quite an impression from a distance. Folks new to the area that see it for the first time, think a conflagration to rival the great Chicago fire is in progress and headed their way. The fire department lists Bob as a potential false alarm source. On nights with ice fog, it's not uncommon for the fire department to call and ask him to turn the production off and on several times so the callers can verify that what they are seeing is, in fact, no threat.

Of course, all of this isn't done without Blizzard Bob having to bear some hardship. He does, after all, have to go through the neighborhood and borrow all those extension cords. I wouldn't mind it so much, but the heat from the lights causes the snow to melt around the displays, and the resultant ice build-up makes it impossible to retrieve the extension cords before spring break up.

The heat has caused other problems as well. When Bob first started putting the displays up, he used birch trees and shrubs. All that warmth got them to budding out by the middle of December, and now all he has left is his spruce (They don't seem to be adversely affected, and I suspect the heat may even be beneficial by luring spruce bark beetles out into the dead of winter).

Knucks Mahoneigh brought up an idea about returning the generosity that Bob displays by purchasing several dozen strings of lights for him. Knucks thought we all ought to chip in and get all the lights Bob could use. His goal was to replace everything Bob was using with the strings that go out when one bulb is bad. The plan was that each day, one of us would slip over and place one bum bulb in each display. Ultimately, we decided it would be too time consuming to go that route, so each year the neighborhood's gift to Blizzard Bob is the same: we forgive him.

What the heck, it's the Christmas season.

You Got a *What*?

Every year there is an odd assortment of gifts that, although appreciated for the thought behind them, are not timely or the best for use in Alaska. These are things sent by well-intentioned relatives from down south.

Everyone gets gifts like these. It's part of the grand tradition. These gifts serve a definite purpose too, they are ever so handy when it comes time at the New Year's Eve party to talk about what sort of booty was received. Sooner or later, someone will mention something off-the-wall that was sent to them, and all other conversations are interrupted with the resultant, "You got a *what*?" From that point on, as one bizarre or useless gift after another is described, all the conversations take a turn for the better. Many a slow New Year's Eve has been salvaged with such an exchange.

Mittens, or mitten and hat combinations, seem to be a staple in the gift category. I sometimes envision how all the local evening news broadcasters throughout the warmer climates of the United States must go on one or two evenings in November, and set this avalanche of mittens in motion.

"This just in from the wire service: people in Alaska have no mittens. Alaska's governor announced a state of emergency today, when the entire winter supply of mittens being shipped to Alaska was lost at sea. This tragic situation came about as the only barge scheduled to deliver mittens for the entire state, capsized and sank.

The Governor described the situation as grim and desperate. If you have any relatives in Alaska, send them mittens for Christmas."

Getting mittens isn't really such a bad thing, but mittens are one of the first things Alaskans purchase in late October, when the lakes freeze up and the snow flies. So, come time for Christmas, sending an Alaskan mittens is like sending a Floridian a crate of oranges.

Another common article of clothing received, is socks. Not the good old ragg wool or beefy wool blend type. Not socks with guts, something with substance and stamina, made for the rigors found in the Last Frontier, but those namby-pamby, tissue thin, stretch-over-the-calf things.

"Isn't that sweet, Dear? Aunt Tildy sent you some nice socks."

"Oooh baby, baby! With these and my wingtips, I'll be the envy of all the other guys out icefishing. Say, you don't suppose that black will clash with my brown cotton duck insulated coveralls do you? If so, we may have a problem."

Of course, to be perfectly honest here, I really don't mind getting a high quality pair of those skinny stretch socks now and then. If you cut a small hole in the toes, they'll slip right over the butt of your fishing rod, and stretch over the reel to protect it from dust while traveling. Additionally, when Aunt Tildy visits, she'll see that they're treasured beyond their useful life as a simple article of clothing.

However, beyond a shadow of a doubt, even worse than the socks themselves, is getting the little elastic garters that hold them up. Apparently, Alaskans have a monopoly on the judicious application of duct tape to keep socks up. Some enterprising soul ought to market a duct tape in the big cities down south that is only one inch wide. Give it a catchy name like "Roll o' garter" and a snazzy package. The young urban professionals would beat a path to the door.

Food items also seem to be something everyone receives. Few are those who haven't been a petrified fruit cake recipient. I swear there are some fruit cakes that are passed around like family heirlooms year after year.

"Good Lord, Johnny! Don't eat that fruit cake. It's been in the family for generations."

Another food item that continually shows up only at Christmas is the Brazil nut. This is truly the gift that says, "I was thinking of you, but not very highly." What are Brazil nuts used for? Has anyone ever seen a recipe that calls for Brazil nuts to be used in any fashion? I think not. Does anyone know how to successfully open a Brazil nut? Does anyone know why one would want to? I would wager that even a raven would pass on Brazil nuts. But every year, there they are, just daring you to try and open them.

Home improvement is a theme most of the relatives that have visited in the past four years have picked up on. One generous uncle sent the entire *This Old House* series on video tape. I watched them for the fine acting only. Frankly, watching that guy contract out all that demolition and rebuilding work made me wonder. Why doesn't he just build a new home? It would be a whole lot quicker, and probably a good deal cheaper. Along with the videos have come several hand saws, hammers, carpenter belts and other building type doodads. Just as soon as I'm done with the carport, I'm gonna have a garage sale.

Some Christmas gifts breed other Christmas gifts. This year's gift from Aunt Tildy was an ice crusher, which was a direct result of last year's gift. When Tildy was up last summer she asked for some creme de menthe over crushed ice "to aid digestion, you know." So, without thinking it through, I set out the bottle of peppermint schnapps and then pulled out the unused half of last year's Christmas gift out, (the other half of the Christmas gift was in use on my fishing rod) stuffed it full of ice, and gave the whole shebang a few good licks with the latest Christmas hammer. To say the least, Aunt Tildy was shocked. In fact, she refused her libation.

I was shocked too. Who would have ever figured she would know the difference between creme de menthe and peppermint schnapps?

I like my schnapps right out of the bottle. I don't know what we're going to do with an ice crusher. Wonder what it would do to Brazil nuts.

The Secret to Getting Through Cabin Fever

In a cordial conversation with just about any tourist, what is one of the first things that they say about Alaskans? More than likely, within the first five minutes of the conversation, the tourist will comment about how friendly Alaskans are. I like that about where we live. We, as Alaskans, are recognized as being friendly folk. On those occasions that my family has drugged, hogtied and forcibly transported me to the Lower Forty-eight for visits, people I don't even know have remarked on how courteously they were treated when visiting the Great Land. A reputation like that is an enviable one.

Our reputation as a friendly place to visit is also the reason that the folks in the tourism industry have to be nuts to try and advance Alaska as a good place to visit in the winter. Winter, although beautiful in many respects, is not the time to try and enjoy our state. It's true that the scenery is just as good, and granted, there are many fantastic winter activity opportunities, but there is also a minor congeniality problem. Alaskans have a late winter personality defect called "cabin fever."

An Alaskan with a good dose of cabin fever makes a pistol whipping, New York subway mugger seem like a smiley-faced chairperson of the local Welcome Wagon committee.

If the winter tourism push continues, I foresee the issuance of U.S. State Department warnings against travel to Alaska during certain winter months. These advisories would be similar to the ones issued for areas with life or health threatening problems such as cholera or violent revolutions and the like. The State of Alaska could end up being quarantined against outside visitors from the middle of February to the end of March.

Modern cabin fever is not brought about entirely as the result of being cooped-up inside for long periods of time, like it used to be in the days of the early homesteaders and pioneers. The current version is much more complex. Modern cabin fever is more of a general irritation, an annoying itch that can't even be identified, let alone scratched.

Standard cabin fever can be alleviated by simply getting out and seeing sights different than the four walls that normally surround you. Unfortunately, in curing standard cabin fever, an entirely new set of irritations are encountered that create our modern cabin fever.

Getting out in itself becomes a great source of aggravation. It involves the use of motorized vehicles to go from one place to another. Immediately upon getting on the road, it becomes apparent that there are only two types of drivers: those in front of you that drive too slow, and those behind you that want to drive too fast and are right on your bumper. Each trip into town is an exercise in developing new and different epithets to describe everyone else on the road.

The purple verbiage that is generated is at times a source of potential embarrassment. After following some flaming idiot for quite a distance at the speed of thirty-five miles an hour on a dry surface, during a bright, clear day, you both turn into a parking lot. Venom is still dripping from your lips as you park next to the individual whose lineage you have just finished speculating to be the most bizarre and unnatural imaginable. You turn to the offending vehicle to shoot the most potent of dagger looks, and your pastor's wife smiles back and waves merrily.

The only thing worse than the road trip amplification of cabin fever, is the lack of opportunity to get it. Nothing will inflame the raw nerves of a winter tired Alaskan worse than jumping in the old car, turning the ignition key, and listening to a battery groan with its last and dying spurt of energy. Even if the car does start, there is no guarantee that you will go anywhere. On particularly cold days, just because the clutch went in, does not necessarily mean it will come back out to initiate transportation.

In the old days, cabin fever was alleviated by hearing from the family down south. Letters would arrive with welcome news about the folks, and what was going on. These would take at least a week to arrive. Now, with instant, and comparatively inexpensive phone communication available, hearing from the folks down south has become yet another cabin fever amplifier. It isn't meant to be, but the typical March phone call from my sister is something that can make a bad day abysmal.

"Hello."

"Hi. I thought I'd call and cheer you up. You're always so grumpy this time of year."

"Thank you for your kind words. What's new?"

"Well, the daffodils are starting to bloom, and we've started working the ground for the vegetable garden. Of course, it is a little early, we could still get a frost... So what have you been doing?"

Deep, slow breaths. Deep, slow breaths. Concentrate! Don't let your voice tremble! "Well, we shoveled the snow off our roof yesterday. That was fun. We're probably going to dig the front door out today, or maybe I'll walk into town for a new car battery."

"Yeah, Mike is out getting some exercise too. He and some of the guys from work are playing golf. Well, just called to cheer you up. Got to get going. I've got to take the kids to the park to sign up for little league. It starts in a couple of weeks, you know. I'll call next week."

"Kathy? I've never mentioned this before, but Mom and Dad actually found you. You aren't really their child."

"Love you too, bye-bye."

All these aggravations can culminate in rough relations with friends and neighbors. A recent spat between a couple of my neighbors, Knucks Mahoneigh and Blizzard Bob, is a prime example.

Knucks and B.B. have been more than just friends and neighbors for years. They are the charter members of the NORSMen (North Road Supportive Men, a support group dedicated to carrying on the male traditions of scratching, spitting and cigar smoking), and even more importantly, hunting and fishing partners. On more than one occasion, during periods of domestic discord, one has sought refuge at the other's house for a night or two. On several occasions, during periods of domestic discord, both have spent cold nights huddled in B.B.'s garage. Basically, these guys are tight.

The argument began over at B.B.'s house, and for some odd reason traveled to my doorstep, where I was drawn into the conflict.

It all apparently started quietly enough at B.B.'s house, over a cup of coffee. B.B. prepared one of his special blends, as he always does. Knucks politely accepted, as he always does, and proceeded to slurp the first sip, which is the only way to enjoy a cup of Bob's lava java and manage to keep one's lips. At this point, cabin fever took over, and B.B. apparently launched into a tirade about how he has *always* hated the way Knucks slurps his coffee.

Knucks started naming a few of Blizzard Bob's flaws. This led to an open exchange of possibly real, but mostly imagined, personal offenses committed against one another since having first met. In the course of this baring of souls, Knucks got up and walked out. Bob followed him, and they ended up arguing on my front walkway, the one I had just finished clearing from all the snow thrown off the roof.

As their gestures became more animated, shoving and slipping ensued. B.B. slipped and tumbled, which created a mini-avalanche from the snow piled along the walk. At that point, all three of our voices were raised, and everyone had their say until nothing was left unsaid, although much should have been.

After a few silent minutes spent standing, puffing and red-faced, we all turned and went our separate ways.

We still get together to sit and glare at one another over a cup of Bob's coffee. After all, that's the real secret in getting through cabin fever: sharing your time with good friends.

Feeling SHAD

I am just one of many people in Alaska that suffers from depression during the bleak periods of winter. Many people are adversely affected by the long hours of darkness and seemingly interminable cold. This type of depression has been given the acronym "SAD," for Seasonal Affective Disorder. This depression is thought to be brought about, in part, by the lack of sunshine, and affects both men and women.

Of course, not everyone who is feeling low is suffering from SAD. Many others have a closely related condition called SHAD, or Spousal House Arrangement Depression. This problem affects mostly men who are married to women that contend with their own depression by rearranging the house constantly in the middle of winter.

Don't get me wrong, change is a good thing. Moving the furniture around now and then can help keep a household from looking stagnant, and will help prevent uneven worn spots in the carpet. A fresh coat of paint on a wall or two can make a drab room look more cheery. However, one must bear in mind that making changes in the home should be like the medicinal application accorded good whiskey: in moderation only. Any over-application of a good thing is a sure cause of headache.

There are varying degrees to SHAD. Not everyone is going to have a severe case of depression. Some will suffer just minor irritation. There are many variables that can affect the problem:

general health, physical conditioning, work-related stress, and just how far your spouse goes in changing the household.

There is a big difference between entering the house one evening and throwing the old hat and gloves into a new, piranha infested fifty-five gallon aquarium instead of on the hallway table. And for instance, walking into the dining room to find the walls stripped bare, little shreds of wallpaper remnants dangling from the corners, large strips strewn across the floor, and your spouse sitting, just staring at the denuded walls in deep contemplation.

The first scenario is only a minor irritation. The hat and gloves can be retrieved safely with a gaff and then dried. Additionally, watching fish has a soothing effect. And don't worry about the cat because after the first bite or two, he'll either learn to keep his paws out, or can be fitted with a little kitty prosthesis of some sort.

The wallpaper situation is cause for genuine depression. The wallpaper will have to be replaced. This means at least one full weekend will be spent with great wailings and gnashing of teeth as the "right" wallpaper is chosen. Another full weekend will be lost while trying to match a pattern. This is a bad situation to be in. The best one can hope for, is to limit the severity of the depression by lightening the work load.

"Looks like you've decided on a change. I like it. Sort of opens up the room."

"Got tired of looking at the same old, boring pattern."

"Well, we've had it for a long time. That old stuff has been around since, what? Last March wasn't it? Let's try some paint this time."

"No, I was thinking maybe a jungle floral pattern."

Massive decor changes aren't the only thing that can bring about SHAD. Bruised shins contribute to the condition. Bruised shins are the result of furniture rearrangement complicated by lack of sunlight which is amplified by our intermittent absence of electrical power when winter storms rage.

It never fails, the first thing a man does when the lights go out is jump up valiantly and declare, "I'll get a flashlight."
The second thing he does is let out a loud string of epithets as he tumbles through the darkness, arms flailing wildly to cushion the fall, when the recently relocated coffee table or foot stool is found.

Sometimes, just a little thing can set off SHAD, something as simple as the hanging of a picture. One day you notice that the picture Uncle Mort personally painted for the family is hanging prominently in a room where it might be seen by visitors. As you recall, the picture had been lovingly admired when received, and then pitched under the house for storage.

"Honey, why did you hang Uncle Mort's picture? Man, this is some butt-ugly painting. Is that mildew, or did he actually intend to use that color?"

"I sort of like it there. Besides, it covers the holes."

SHAD envelops you like a cold, suffocating mist. "Holes? What holes? When did we get holes?"

"I didn't want to hang that particular picture, I wanted a little one, but I couldn't get the picture to hang right, so I used a bigger nail. Then I missed with the hammer and knocked a hole in the wall. It still wasn't right, so I moved it over and tried again. Then ... well, it doesn't look *that* bad. Does it?"

What can be done about SHAD? Exercise? No, somebody with SHAD gets plenty of exercise painting, moving furniture, laying carpet and so forth. Getting out, around town? No, because when you have SHAD, lots of trips to town are in order for supplies. It seems the only real help for SHAD is a good support group.

This year, I feel better, and so do my neighbors Blizzard Bob (B.B.) and Knucks Mahoneigh. We formed our own support group. We decided to call it NORSMen, for North Road Supportive Men. We picked that name because it's really kind of catchy. Visions of super macho, Viking kinda guys slurping down pickled herring and swilling beer immediately spring up.

Blizzard Bob is the one who came up with the idea. He read the dust cover on a book about guys bonding and being macho together, and just sort of figured it was the ticket to help fight SHAD.

The NORSMen meet in B.B.'s garage once a week. We chose his place because he hasn't cleaned it, let alone rearrange anything, for years. If there's a power outage, we know to walk around the workbench, step over the lawnmower, and duck under the ten-speed hanging from the ceiling. Exactly two more steps to the right, and there's the cooler. Who needs a flashlight?

Mostly we just sit around, maybe do a little scratching and spitting, incinerate a few cigars, and just in general act manly. But sometimes we really do discuss problems. Deep problems. Like, how thin can the wallpaper glue be made, and still do the job? Is it better to spackle in layers, or glob it on, and then sand it down? Who sells the best paint in town? And of course, the question that burns in the minds of all men: how long should a bruised shin be iced?

Winter Brr-beque

Traditions come in all manner and fashion. Usually a tradition is carried out to mark some point in time, be it large or small, by performing a ritual. The ritual simply has to have a preset time frame. It doesn't necessarily have to make any sort of sense to anyone, even those that observe the tradition.

Late January is the time for traditions that help to mark the passing of winter. Things like trips outside to warmer climates are big right now. In late February, one of the most popular traditions to mark the passing of winter will begin with the annual mass migration to Anchorage to celebrate "Fur Rondy." But who wants to wait until late February? The third week in January marks an important point: less than ninety days of winter remain before spring break-up is assured.

These sort of traditions are important in keeping the winter blahs at bay.

Quietly ignoring winter's psychological battering by turning your back and flying away to warmth and sunshine is fine. Seeking diversion by running off to the big city is also acceptable. However, I prefer to stand my ground and spit in winter's eye; after carefully checking the wind's direction, of course. This is a point of honor, a matter of pride, a way to show that the rigors of winter haven't beaten me. It is time for the traditional "Winter Countdown Kickoff Barbeque."

It's more than just a way to brighten the weekend. It's a bona fide slap in the face to old man winter. What better way to assert defiance to winter than with a summer activity?

Of course, anything as important as declaring psychological war on winter is likely to demand a little effort, and there are a few minor difficulties associated with this ritual.

The biggest drawback to the whole affair is that the celebration always seems to coincide with the coldest weather of the winter. There could be a sweep of unseasonably warm temperatures the day before the barbeque, but on the day of the big event, a howling norther will bring on a good imitation of an uninhabited ice planet. This is part of the tradition; winter doesn't pass quietly, and takes exception to those of us that would hurry it along.

It is imperative to maintain a good attitude. Reasoning is everything. For example: you need the parka to keep your clothes from smelling like smoke, and the mittens are to keep from burning your hands. Also, one doesn't want to stand outside too long just in case there might be a mosquito problem.

Another minor difficulty is the barbeque grill. If you should happen to be one of those rare people that are always organized and well prepared, the grill will be right where you put it last fall: in the storage shed. However, normal folk have to hunt around a little to find their grills. The best way to locate a grill in the off season is to identify the largest mound of snow on or near the back porch. Look for the really big pile that was made when shoveling off the roof. The grill will be found exactly in the middle of that pile.

During the grill excavation is the perfect time to give some thought as to what should be barbequed. Common sense would dictate that hotdogs be the choice. They can be thrown on and done in less time than it takes to get minor frostbite on your smaller extremities, but we're talking tradition, not common sense.

The whole point to the barbeque is not simply to celebrate the demise of winter, but to show utter contempt for it. Something that takes a long time to cook is needed. Something that is generally reserved for the summer. A thick, juicy roast is just the thing. A roast and potato salad is just the meal to drive home the point that winter is on its way out.

With the grill dug out and the meal planned, it's time for the traditional lighting of the mid-winter barbeque fire.

Grab that old bag of summer charcoal. When the bottom drops out, throw the bag away and pick the briquettes out of the snow, piling them carefully in the grill. It will be necessary to apply at least a double dose of lighter fluid. Don't worry if the lighter fluid looks like hair gel, it'll still burn if it's preheated with large amounts of flaming newspaper. With the blazing heat of summer started, it's time to go inside and peel off that hot protective gear.

To help pass the time while the coals get going, practice traditional summer sayings.

"Fish on!"

"Hey batter-batter swing!"

"Pass the bug dope, please."

"Who ate the last piece of watermelon?"

Another really good Winter Countdown Kickoff Barbeque pastime is trying to remember all the lyrics to "Crazy Days of Summer" or, even better, Mungo Jerry's great summer season classic "In the Summertime." Make it a family sing-along.

By the time the last chorus echoes off the walls amid the kids' harmonic laughter, the coals will be ready. Now is the time for action. Put your protective barbeque gear back on, and rush outside with roast dangling from fork. Throw the roast on the grill and close the lid before the whole thing fills up with snow. Now, go back inside to find a beer or cold soda. No summer barbeque is complete without the balance of drink in one hand and fork in the other.

After giving the roast a few minutes to get going, it's time to check the progress. Put your protective gear back on, grab your drink, and casually saunter back outside to see how things are going.

Two things will be readily evident. First, what was just a refreshing thirty or forty knot breeze will have changed to a serious wind. This is perfectly normal. It's a result of the updraft from the grill. Secondly, there will be no smoke rising from the vents. This is because there are no vents visible under the drifted snow.

Maintaining total indifference to the raging, howling ground blizzard, mosey over to the grill and check out the situation. The roast will be done average medium: scorched on the bottom, frozen on top. A quick call to the house is in order, "Honey, it's ready. Time to heat up the oven."

Keeping the Home Fires Burning

Every year during March, three things are inevitable: all schools will be closed for a week during spring break, many families will migrate to warm, sunny parts of the world, and Blizzard Bob will be asked to watch Knucks Mahoneigh's house while Knucks and his family soak up sunshine.

It's not that Bob couldn't go someplace warm for a vacation this time of year-- he just doesn't want to. March frequently provides up to half of the annual snowfall in southcentral Alaska. B.B. wouldn't want to miss the opportunity to get in some serious recreational snow relocation. Additionally, B.B. is rewarded for his caretaking efforts with lavish gifts.

He summed up his reasoning for not vacationing in March this way, "We're talkin' prime snowblowin' bud! Besides, Knucks always brings me back a little something. Once, he gave me a really clever cigarette dispenser that looks like a donkey. Just lift the tail... and there you go! Of course, we don't smoke, but it is a good conversation piece."

But this year is going to be different. Knucks and his family are staying home because Bob's performance as the lone sentry last year was less than acceptable by most accounts. With Knucks and his family gone, Bob had found himself with a list of things to do. There were cats to feed and clean the litter box after, as the Mahoneighs don't let them outside. There were lizards and the fish to feed. Plants to water in the middle of the week. There was also Grrr, Knucks' dog.

Grrr is a malemute mix that generally likes everybody and everything, except Bob. Over the course of the previous years, Bob had learned to give Grrr as much room as he wants. Watering and feeding him while Knucks was on vacation had become a ritual of quick moves. The first step was to get Grrr's attention, which was never hard to do, as he would be straining against his chain in a vain attempt to get Bob in his jaws. Bob would show Grrr a large dog biscuit, and then throw it to the other side of the chain's length. This would allow Bob the opportunity to dash in and grab the dishes. After refilling them, he would push them back into Grrr's reach with a long pole.

Everything went fine until the third day. One of the fish wasn't acting right. Bob couldn't claim to be an expert, but it seemed to him that a fish shouldn't swim upside down. No doubt about it, that fish was a goner. Nothing to do but give it the big flush.

He scooped the fish up with a net, carried it into the bathroom, and put it in the toilet. As soon as the fish hit the water, it started swimming around. Bob was now faced with a moral dilemma: send what now appeared to be a healthy fish to its doom, or return it to the tank with its brethren, and possibly infect them all? He mulled it over and decided to take a wait and see attitude. The fish certainly wasn't going anywhere. Besides, it didn't appear that the net would fit down to the bottom of the bowl, and Bob had always been shy about groping around in other people's toilets with his hands.

Things didn't go well with the lizards either. The instructions said to feed them on Tuesday. The note mentioned nothing about the food jumping out of the box. When Bob opened the lid, only three of the dozen or so crickets failed to make good their escape. Mahoneigh's were in Hawaii, maybe they'd bring back some geckos.

On the fourth day the plants were supposed to be watered. Unfortunately, kitty anarchy had ruled the night before, and there wasn't enough dirt left in the pots to hold even a teaspoon of water. Bob scooped up as much dirt as he could off the floor, but couldn't recover enough to fill even one pot. With all four plants in one pot, it sure made for a nice, thick display.

On the fifth day, for the first time ever, the diversionary feeding tactic didn't work on Grrr. Bob threw the biscuit too far, and Grrr had come to an abrupt and unpleasant halt. Between the recoil and Grrr's intense desire to get even, Bob found himself just half a leg short of a clean escape. No serious damage was incurred, but he could have sworn Grrr actually smiled.

Day six was uneventful, except as he left, Bob noticed the front porch light he left on at night was burned out. No problem. He'd get a light bulb from home and put it in the next morning so the light would be on when Knucks and his family got home in the evening.

Other than the fish, a few crickets running loose, the loss of a little potting soil and a chewed up pants leg, everything had gone very well.

Saturday. The Mahoneigh's would be home by nine that evening. Bob wondered what Knucks would bring him. (Secretly, he hoped it would be one of those pens that show a girl in a bikini when you turn it upside down.) He stepped up on the porch and changed out the light bulb. It didn't light. Must have left the switch off.

Stepping into the house, Bob knew there was a problem. Why could he see his breath floating in the air? The drooping pot of plants indicated it was close to freezing.

A glance out the back door showed the situation in a nutshell. An old birch had finally given up the battle with gravity, and had taken out the power connection to the house. It had probably happened just prior to his visit the day before.

The cats were fine. The lizards were a different story. If not so macabre, they would have made interesting broaches. A quick dash to the bathroom showed that the water in the toilet was not frozen, but the fish had assumed an inverted view of the world.

Bob's main concern at this point was to save the water pipes in the house. He decided to get a fire going in the wood stove in the family room, then call the electric company to see about hooking the power back up.

With the fire going strong, Bob called the electric company. He had just gotten to the point where he was giving directions to the house when the roaring in the stovepipe increased to a deafening level.

"I've gotta go!"

"Yes sir, what is your location?"

"I've gotta go, *now!*"

"Sir, if you want a repair crew to..."

"Lady, get off the phone! I've got a fire to report!"

When Knucks got home that evening, he found a note pinned to the door: "Please don't go in before you see me -- Bob."

Knucks did indeed get Bob a bikini girl pen, but he kept it for himself to fill out all the insurance claims.

Big Parade

The big plot of land between Airport Way and the Dairy Queen just sat there, scraped clean, for two years.

"Gonna build a big store there. We're just not sure what kind yet."

Rumors and factual reports flew until the new official announcement came out. "Nevermind, no we're not."

Finally, after two years of yes we are/no we're not, someone decided to actually do something with the lot. It was decided to put in a new Carr's Grocery store. Still, the lot sat pretty much unchanged for most of the summer after Carr's told the world of their bold plan. When fall arrived, there was a flurry of activity, and a parking lot and a foundation took shape. As the snow started to fly, a building started up, and a completion date was set for April 4th.

Through the first part of winter, progress was noticeable on the outside, and then most of the activity was concentrated on the inside.

Nothing this exciting had happened in Kenai since the first traffic lights were put up in 1988, so it wasn't surprising that the topic of a new, bigger, better grocery store seemed to creep into almost all conversations. It became an obsession with my wife. She delivered daily reports about the progress, and what would happen next in regards to the new store.

83

"You know what I heard today? There's even going to be a sushi bar."

"No kidding? I had no idea that sushis even drank. Imagine that."

"I'm serious. It's going to be huge. There'll be a deli, fresh seafood, a great, big bakery, flowers..."

"Sounds like the first order of business for shopping there will be to buy provisions for the excursion. I can hear it now: *Search and Rescue to aisle five, we have a lost shopper somewhere between the cantaloupe and the kiwi fruit.*"

I couldn't match her breathless enthusiasm for a new store, but did have to admit, something different might take some of the drudgery out of scrounging up the family victuals. However, when she announced there was going to be a parade to mark the grand opening, I wrote it off as being just too bizarre.

"A parade? Get outta my face. For a *grocery store*?"

"No, really. They're going to have a parade from the old store to the new one."

"You mean there'll be a convoy of trucks to move the stock."

"No. I mean a parade. You know, where everyone marches down the road in gala celebration of some noteworthy event."

"Oh, moose pucky."

Now, I have watched TV early on New Year's Day. I know what a parade is. Still, I had a hard time envisioning what a parade for a grocery store would encompass. The more I thought about it, the more peculiar the visions became.

The first thing that came to mind was that everyone in the community would join in by taking a canned good to march down the Spur Highway. "Okay, everyone with the sixteen ounce succotash, head out, followed by the asparagus and creamed corn. All right, look sharp. Here we go!"

Of course, no parade would be complete without a band. That would be the responsibility of the Personal Care department in the form of tissue paper and comb kazoos.

Logistics got in the way of that particular scenario. There was no way all the cans could be stocked properly once the parade arrived at the new store. A celebration, not mayhem, is the object of a parade.

The idea of each department marching over in costumes rolled through the empty expanse of my mind. The bakery folks could dress like croissants or bagels or even cream puffs. The produce department could go dressed like giant cabbage heads, dancing bananas, celery stalks and whatnot. The meat section could be led by a cow. Of course the dairy section could also be led by a cow, but the meat department's cow wouldn't have any legs, to signify ground beef.

Finally, the big day arrived. The parade was to kick off at eight-thirty in the morning. Driving into town, I couldn't believe that there were people actually lining the streets. To watch a parade for a *grocery store*?

The old store's parking lot was full of paraders. We drove on down to the new store and parked. Not wanting to miss the full impact of the parade, we walked down to the corner of the Spur Highway and Main Street Loop.

It was there that my first thought struck me: the cop in the street is probably one of the very few law enforcement officers in the country whose job has entailed traffic control for a parade to celebrate the opening of a new *grocery store*.

The parade itself was nothing like the visions my imagination had conjured up. It was pretty much your run-of-the-mill parade. The procession was led by the various Carr's dignitaries in suits and sneakers, carrying a "GRAND OPENING" banner. They were followed by classic automobiles from the local auto club, the local high school bands, the Junior Majorettes Club, beauty queens, and clowns. In fact, the whole thing could have been passed off as a Fourth of July parade except there weren't any political candidates throwing candy at the kids, school buses or Peninsula Sanitation refuse trucks.

At midway in the parade, the second thought struck me: I know or recognize most of these people. We are all standing around, in ten degree weather, cheering a parade for a *grocery store*.

As the parade passed, we fell in line with a group of friends and neighbors, all of us laughing at ourselves for being at a parade for a grocery store. All of us eager to get inside and have a look for ourselves at this miracle of modern shopping convenience.

The store was big, and it was packed with people. It took close to forty minutes to wind our way from one end to the other. Not just because the store is so big, or that the crowds were so thick, but because it seemed half the people there were friends, and a chat with each was required. It was a party with shopping carts.

Standing at the far corner of the store, waiting for a six-pack of tuna rolls at the sushi bar, a little cluster of people passed by me. I could tell they weren't local. They were dressed like they had just climbed down from Mt. McKinley in January. They were talking among themselves. One fellow, fully decked out in an impeccable L.L. Bean parka, said in a derisive manner, "It's obvious the locals are hurting for entertainment."

At that point, my third and final thought for the day (I only allow myself three, it gets too scary with more than that) struck me: this isn't just about the opening of a grocery store. It's about being a community.

May that man in the parka someday be as lucky as we are.

Mail Disorder

It is never so apparent that Alaskans are separate from the rest of the country as during national spring sale catalog time. It seems as if there is a daily reminder in the mail that most of the rest of the country is about to roll into spring. I'm talking about all the "Big Bonanza Spring Sale!" catalogs that choke off the flow of important mail, starting in early March.

There is nothing that seems so out of place as a catalog extolling the virtues of a certain brand of summer apparel on a day that might get as warm as ten degrees. But it's not just clothing catalogs that pour in. There are catalogs for just about anything that could be used in three or four months after they arrive: fishing and camping gear, summer action wear, and my favorite, the beachwear selections.

"Hey, Hon? The new swim suit catalog is in."

"Oh goody! We'll have just enough time to order something to wear on the first clam digging trip. When is the first good clam tide anyway?"

"April fifteenth."

The biggest advantage to mail order catalogs is that items can be purchased before it would make any sense to display them locally. This affords the mail order shopper a luxury that a store shopper doesn't have: the opportunity to mull over the purchase before plunking down cold cash. If a store shopper takes a few days to think about their purchase, it might be too late to consummate the deal.

"Hi there. I was in just a couple of days ago, looking at a summer outfit that was mostly a flower pattern with checker and stripe patches and a purple polka dot border. I couldn't decide if it would go with my orange gingham jacket... It was right in this area. Do you still have it?"

"Sorry, it's gone. Had to get rid of the summer stuff to make room for all the fall fashions. Could I interest you in a nice parka in a floral pattern?"

Another reported advantage to mail order shopping is the reduced cost. These savings are really just hypothetical. If all one had to pay was the listed price, everything would be great, but there's always shipping charges.

"Okay, ma'am, that's two Buffalo plaid shirts, the size ten Easy Walker striding shoes, two pairs of Happy Yachtsman shorts, two Carefree Breezes summer dresses, and the chartreuse, high visibility, clam digger bikini. That will come to eighty-eight dollars, plus shipping. Will that be COD or charge?"

"Uh, wait a minute. What'll the shipping be?"

"What's your zip code?"

"It's nine-nine-six-three-five."

"That's a new one on me. Nine-nine-six... Uh-oh. You're in *Alaska*? I'll have to get out my special shipping charges book."

What it all boils down to is that for the price of slightly more than it took to lay the Alaska Pipeline, eight pounds of clothing can be shipped by air in something less than a month.

However, if you're really out to save money, into gambling, and aren't hung up on things like time frames, the order can be shipped by the ambiguous term of "surface freight."

It is important to note that this mode of transportation is not given a specific, descriptive term like, for instance, "truck" or even "mule train." This is because the shipper isn't quite sure exactly how the order will be moved. All they know for certain is that somehow, the order will travel across the surface of the earth.

I sometimes think orders that come from down south in this manner don't really have any scheduled routes. The charges you pay go to somebody that waits at a roadside stop and tries to pass along your goodies to somebody else that may, or may not, be headed this way.

"Say buddy, you headed up to Alaska? Well, how far north are you going? Would you mind throwing this on top of your car? Yeah, when you get to Missoula, just drop it off with somebody there that's headed north. Naw, you don't have to hang around 'til someone actually picks it up. Just leave it with a note; there's an address on the package. It'll make it... maybe."

Even if there were some sort of significant savings when ordering through the mail, it's not like the stuff is of any better quality than what you'd buy locally. Particularly in the case of electronic items, where it's still the basic warranty of ninety days.

"Hello, Arcanflame Electronics."

"Yes. I'd like to return the Bleepin' Fishfinder I ordered from your company for repairs under warranty. Order number six-six-three-seven."

"Oh gee, I'm sorry, but that warranty is expired. Our records show that you purchased that fish locator in February."

"Yeah, but it just got here last week."

"Well, it's almost June... That's more than ninety days. You can send it to our factory shop for repairs, if you'd like. May I make a suggestion? You can save a lot on shipping if you send it by surface freight."

It seems the only certain guarantee after placing an order through the mail is that your mailbox will be straining at the seams from the resultant deluge of additional catalogs.

Another problem with ordering by mail is getting the wrong size, color or model. Worse yet is trying to return something that just doesn't live up to your expectations. Just try and return that puppy. Mail order operators have the perfect stone wall defense in the form of questions. When putting up this defense they never actually tell you that the item cannot be returned, it's just something that is quickly deduced.

"Hello, I'd like to return an item I ordered through your company."

"Is it the wrong item?"

"No, not exactly..."

"The wrong size, perhaps?"

"Well, no, not exactly, it's..."

"Then the item is defective in some manner?"

"No, no, it's not that, it's just that it..."

"Well then, if it's not defective, not the wrong item, or not the wrong size, then there really isn't anything wrong with it, and there's no need to return it, is there?"

"Yes there is. This doesn't look a thing like it's supposed to. This thing is damned butt-ugly!"

"Very well sir, if you'll just return that to us by air freight, we'll get your $15.25 refund off to you right away by surface freight. Will that be all?"

You'd better believe it.

Spring Thing

By late March, it becomes apparent that there will be an end to winter. Sure, there might be a few last snowstorms in April to set the progress back a few days, but the increasing solar energy is an undeniable force. Things must warm up, simply because there is more time with radiant heat, than without. The longer, warmer days loosen winter's grip, and the snow starts to slip away.

The receding snow turns spring into a time of discovery. Misplaced items are found, questions are answered and great truths are revealed as the veil of winter melts away.

Anyone who feeds birds over the course of a winter wonders how the little critters can eat so much seed. It isn't uncommon to fill a feeder full of sunflower seeds in the morning, before leaving for work, and have the feeder sitting empty upon returning in the evening. Granted, the birds that stay the winter travel in flocks, but two pounds of sunflower seeds divvied up between twenty, little, one or two ounce birds is an amazing amount. One would expect delicate chirping to be replaced with reverberating belches.

As the snow recedes, the amazement over the birds' voracity is replaced with irritation. Mounds of seeds are left behind, piled under the feeder. It becomes apparent that a band of little wastrels has been hosted throughout the winter. Leftovers are in order for next year's little beggars.

Spring can't arrive without the official, annual retrieval of the lost glove. Flattened beyond anything that could be accomplished through mere human effort, the lost mate is peeled off the ground as soon as the miniature glacier retreats from the driveway. The perfectly good, essentially unused other half of the pair sat the winter out in the protected comfort of a drawer or shelf. The reunited pair looks nothing like a matched set. One is thick, supple and inspires warmth just to look at it. The other is wider by half again, and has been pressed to the thickness of newspaper.

Various efforts to make such a pair of gloves match again have been attempted at our house. The best results, to date, have been attained by soaking the undamaged glove in water overnight, and then driving over it repeatedly. However, success has been limited. The artificially treated glove always remains noticeably thicker.

Spring is the time for change. This is never more apparent than when the ice disappears in parking lots. Pennies, nickels, dimes and quarters abound. As the ice layers peel away from the blacktop, it isn't impossible to go shopping for the week's groceries and come out money ahead. On sunny, warm days that promote rapid melting, the parking lots around stores are packed. Easily half the drivers are lured to the lots by the thought of free change, rather than the possibility of spare change.

Where the accumulation of snow has been enhanced by removal efforts, the chances of finding something interesting during the melt are also enhanced. This is particularly true of the berms along the roads.

Every winter a multitude of hidden surprises accumulate along the roadways. When the berms begin to shrink a veritable lost and found stretches for miles. Most of the stuff is simply garbage, some of it is valuable, and on occasion, some of the things poking out of the dripping edges are macabrely inspirational.

One spring, over the course of a week, I watched the subject of the following poem emerge from a berm along a road. (For those of you with a musical bent, this works well with the old country classic, "Ghost Riders in the Sky", so feel free to just sing right out. The chorus between stanzas would go: "Heeeeyyyy Fidooooooo, where'd you goooooo? Berm runners in the spring.")

Berm Runners in the Spring

From out of melting icicles, a patch of fur appears.
At first it's just the eyes and nose, but eventually the ears.
You'll finally learn where Fido went, when he did not return:
He spent the winter frozen stiff within a roadside berm.

Protruding paws outstretched to wave at every passing car,
His tail is stuck in snow and ice, he can't run very far.
A frozen snarl is on his lips to greet the birds that fly
And land upon his frigid snout, to pick out both his eyes.

Standing high on crusty ridge, he strikes a stoic pose
An icon of fidelity amid the melting snows.
Back arrow straight, stretched out full stride, he goes no nowhere
real fast.
The race he's run is over now that winter time has passed.

As the springtime sun grows warmer, it starts to take its toll,
The snow base at his feet recedes; poor Fido starts to roll.
And soon enough our furry friend is one pathetic pup:
The snowbank sloughs and all that's seen is four paws sticking up.

Out of sight, down in a ditch, he finds his resting place,
Defrosted fully, soft and limp, there'll hardly be a trace;
A tuft of fur, perhaps a chain, is all that will remain,
Until next spring when berms are high, and the runners come
out again.

Indoor Plants

March is a bleak month. Outside, there are no vital signs to indicate life other than the occasional soprano raven. However, it's not just what is happening outside that creates a mood of melancholy. Things are pretty nip and tuck inside, too.

It's funny, but true, that the month when spring officially arrives for the Northern Hemisphere, is when fall sets in on the house plants. It's bad enough that every plant outside looks dead, but being subjected to watching all the plants inside curl up and fall apart, makes it almost unbearable. March marks the end of winter, and the end of an arduous and continual struggle to keep the house plants alive.

The first Alaskan house plant we ever had was given to us by friends that had already been through a few Alaskan winters. They gave it to us in late May, but assured us that it would be an indispensable item when the bleak period of time from December through April arrived.

That plant was a puny thing. It was a single shoot of purple passion with three or four leaves. Our benefactors advised us to give it as much sunlight as possible, and water it frequently.

All through summer, that plant grew at an alarming rate. It required repotting on a weekly basis. It hung in the corner of the kitchen in the trailer, and by the end of August, dominated the room.

It was a deep, fuzzy purple testimony to what Alaska's long summer sunlight hours can do for plant life.

Then came the winter months.

At first, the plant was indeed a comforting reassurance that not everything was frozen solid; that all life had not ceased to exist. Then, things got ugly. The leaves started to pale out, turning from a deep and fuzzy purple to a sort of balding, sickly maroon. The heavily foliated stems started to thin out. First, it was just a leaf or two. Then, as if on cue during the first week of March, everything let loose.

One morning I walked into the kitchen, and there was a crunch with every footstep.

"Whoa! Who spilled the box of bran flakes? What a mess."

"Those aren't bran flakes. They're dead leaves... look."

Glancing over at the corner, I saw what appeared to be a hanging pot with maroon colored spaghetti dangling out of it, hanging in odd, twisted shapes. One or two withered leaves clung desperately to the end of each strand.

So went the first of many death Marches.

We have run the full range of available house plants since that first winter, and we have discovered there is nothing that we can't kill. It matters not how hearty or how expensive the stock is, there will be no plant survival past March in our household.

After numerous attempts at the usual plants found in homes, we decided that maybe something more tree like would provide success.

Weeping figs were the first to be tried. Things were looking pretty good until, you guessed it, March. When the third month of the year rolled around, we found that those pricey little shrubs were called weeping fig, not so much because of how they look, but rather because of what you do when they die.

We tried growing an avocado from a pit we'd saved. This was highly touted in a magazine as an easy, inexpensive way to get plants into your home. Our experience left me wondering how avocados have survived as a species.

When we finally got it to grow, it had a trunk the width of a toothpick, with the length of a ponderosa. It stretched ever upward, and sprouted one leaf; the weight of which caused the trunk to fold over and break. This took most of the winter... until March.

A small glimmer of hope was offered in the form of an air fern. Those little wonders need no soil, and aren't all that fond of strong light. They seemed like the answer to all our problems. All they need is to hang in an area with moisture in the air. We bought six.

Moist air is a rare commodity in a winter time Alaskan home: five died with the first drying cold snap. The sixth was placed in the bathroom, so it could get all that moisture from showers. The only problem being, with teenagers in the house, the shower runs constantly. There is, indeed, such a thing as too much moisture: the last air fern succumbed to mildew.

As a desperate attempt to get something, anything, to grow in the house, a Chia Pet was purchased. It turned on us. It got brown and mean. We took it to a nursery to be put down.

The demise of all our plant life can't be attributed entirely to winter; some of the damage is inflicted by cats.

Outside plants only have to worry about hares, birds, moose, root maggots and the like. House plants have it tougher, they have to worry about cats. Cats are the modern house plant's locust plague.

Someone told me when cats chew on your plants, it means they need more vegetable matter to eat. It was suggested that we fill a garden starter box with potting soil and plant an herbal mixture in it. The idea was to just let the cats graze over the herbs to get the needed roughage. Right. You know what a cat thinks a square box of dirt on the floor is for? This was not only a bad idea, but proved cats couldn't care less about whether the litter is "trackless"or not.

Still, after all these years, every fall we load up the house with vegetation that will slowly perish. It becomes a part of the daily routine to talk to the plants, asking them to please not give up. As winter progresses we are reduced to pleading. Toward the end of it all, my relationship with the plants starts to take on the appearance of an old James Cagney film. I'm reduced to begging the plants to just hang on for a few more days, help is on the way, and so forth. It's pathetic.

In the end, March always wins, and the plant remnants are pitched out onto the mound with all the others. We are developing quite a peat bog next to the house.

Really, I guess it's just as well that all the house plants die in March: we need some place to start all the plants we'll kill in the yearly Spring Garden Ritual.

Gardening in Alaska

Every March, the same ritual is performed around our house, the Spring Sacrifice of Fertility. It is a complicated and lengthy ritual, involving specific steps designed to achieve the total destruction of fertile seeds.

The ritual starts with a trip to one of the innumerable stores in the area that has a cardboard display stand with every sort of seed imaginable. The packets on display are an indication as to what type of gardener buys them. Each envelope is covered with brightly colored pictures of the potential flowers. Obviously, if the would-be horticulturist really knew what he or she was doing, the pictures wouldn't be necessary, just the name would suffice. But such is the lure of taking part in the natural cycle of cultivating something live. It attracts even those of us who possess neither skill nor knowledge.

Once the seeds are purchased, the real decisions come into play. What type of germination system should be employed? The choices are even more varied than the seed types. You have your simple plastic bubble packs, your plastic bubble packs with snap-on lid, the gray tray with divider, the plastic sheet with bubble pack inserts, the pressed moss pots, the tear-away moss six-packs, the window sill greenhouse with automated lunar-cycle-activated hydroponics root fertilizer system and so forth. The best decision is simple: buy the most sophisticated and expensive system you can afford with a second mortgage, so you can brag about it to your other gardening friends.

With seeds and pots tightly in fist, something is needed to fill in the gaps. Once again, the choices are seemingly limitless. Just about any potting soil will do, but the "vacuum factor" should be considered. (Vacuum factor is a number derived by multiplying the average hourly labor charges of the local carpet cleaners by the cubic feet per pound of the potting soil.) Potting soil that has the words "natural peat" or "sifted" on the bag should be avoided. These types of soils have a high "vacuum factor."

Another consideration is cost. It's okay to brag about how much you paid for your germination system, but you must get a good deal on your potting soil. After all, dirt is dirt. You will need twice as much soil as you have room for in your pots. Potting soil shrinks after wetting. Potting soil is the wool of the dirt world.

Once all the necessary supplies have been carried home, it's time to start the work of laying out the "indoor forty." Plants need lots of light. This usually means the location of choice for setting up all this potential foliage is the back of the living room couch or on the kitchen table. Either way, your efforts are sure to be the center of conversation.

"Dear, pass the salt please. I believe it's behind that row of Hemerocallis fulva's."

After the seedlings have had a couple of weeks to grow, it's time to thin them. Many rules of thumb and techniques are applied to thinning. Some folks thin with scissors, some simply pinch off the unwanted seedlings with their fingernails. Many people take all but one seedling per starting pot, some leave two. I prefer a natural selection method: set the plants on the floor overnight, and let the cat make the decisions.

By late March, a promising garden is starting to take shape in the household. Between the cat and myself, we have whittled the needed garden acreage down considerably. With each passing day, the sun grows more prominent in the sky, and the promise of a hearty harvest is in the offing. By April, the seedlings have grown beyond belief. They have stretched, straining upward toward the life-giving sun. They now resemble bean sprouts on steroids.

By this time, each morning starts with a healthy watering and a little chat. The kids really enjoy watching the old man talk to his plants. Particularly when I'm reduced to begging the few remaining seedlings not to die.

One by one, the seedlings drape themselves over the edge of the pots in the limp repose of death. By the middle of May, as the ground begins to thaw completely, one to four unidentified seedlings remain. (I never know what plants actually make it, because the labels are lost in the shuffle of throwing out their deceased brethren.)

It is time to "harden" the plants by setting them outside during warm days. The shock of warm to cool to warm usually proves to be the *coup de grace*, but this year was different.

This year was the year of triumph. The year of agrarian victory. I had a record setting total of three plants make it into the ground. I hope the moose enjoyed them.

Next year, when selecting seeds, I'm going to check the guaranteed germination rate on the packets. I'm shopping until I find a guaranteed germination rate of no more than ninety-five percent. That way, I'll only have to kill ninety-five out of one hundred seeds; saving me five percent of necessary effort expended.

Even better, I think, would be if some enterprising seed company would come out with a special "Irradiated, Sterile Seeds" series. That way, those of us with blight laden thumbs and a high moose population density could go through all the motions without any of the inherent gut-wrenching anticipation and ultimate disappointment.

Breakin' Up Is Hard To Do

What a glorious month April is. April means that March is over. March, although a necessary evil to arrive at April, is probably the least appreciated month of the year. March is like a Christmas present from Grandma. It's good only because once it's over, you can get into the neat stuff.

April is important because it signifies the beginning of that which truly sets Alaska apart from the rest of the country: a fifth season. We have the usual, mundane seasons of spring, summer, fall, and winter just like everywhere else, but we have an extra season in the form of break-up to boot.

The rest of the seasons are pretty much the same here as any place else. In spring, the flowers are fussed over, the buds on whatever the moose may have left behind are carefully watched, and each day is counted until school is out. In the summer, everyone gets excited about the warm weather, mowing lawns, going fishing and so forth. In the fall, there's the leaves turning, hunting and all that. In the winter, there's much ado over the snow, skiing, snowmobiling and other diversions.

Break-up is neither winter, nor spring. It's too warm for winter, and too snowy for spring. Break-up is a bona fide season all unto itself. It is a season of bizarre weather. At this particular point in time, it's common to have sun, snow and rain; not just during the same day, but simultaneously. This time of year, if a person looks out the window to determine what to wear, they might be inclined to dress like a Miami flasher, sporting sunglasses, a knit cap and a trenchcoat over shorts.

103

No less weird than the weather, is how people act. Where else in the country would people be found standing around, all excited about a minuscule, suspected patch of mud?

"Look! Look! We've got a patch of mud in the driveway!"

"Get outta here! It's just the first week of April."

"No, I mean it. Really! Kids, come look."

At this point, the entire clan circles the suspected patch of mud.

"See? Right there. It's mud. Good old terra gooey."

"No way, Dad. That's just where a fendercicle fell off the car."

"No, it isn't. A fendercicle would make a mound. This is in a depression. See?"

The entire family is bent over, straining their eyes to discern the identity of the mystery patch when a slight breeze aids in positive identification.

"Stupid dog! Got me excited there for a minute; thought we were about to shift into spring."

The really tough thing about break-up is declaring when it officially starts. With all the other seasons, there is a definite, preset date to mark the occasion. The assigned date may not fall right in line with the season, but there is a spot on the calendar reserved just for that season to begin.

With no absolute date to confirm the existence of break-up, people are left to their own devices to determine the date of the official kickoff. Normally, things melt just a little, and everybody gets excited enough to declare it to be break-up. The next thing you know, winter takes one last, desperate shot. The temperatures plummet down to zero, but the break-up mentality has been set in motion. This usually occurs right around the last week of March or the first week of April.

"Honey, don't you think you ought to put on your coat, and something else besides sneakers?"

"I don't care if it is ten below. April's here, and by golly that means break-up has started. The sun'll warm things up."

Although temperatures can be a good way to gauge the start of break-up, there are some absolute markers for positive identification.

One positive identifier of break-up is the wonderful feeling of discovery that takes place. As the sterile grip of winter recedes, and the world around teeters on the edge of rebirth, wondrous revelations come to all.

"I'll be. I wondered where all those snow shovels were. Must have left them there when I tried to dig out the barbeque in January."

The wild, heady exhilaration felt can lead to perception problems. I once stood at the end of my drive, staring at a patch of brown lawn for almost an hour. The vision of what would soon be a lush covering of neatly trimmed vegetation pulsed through my mind. New, green blades would push up from the dead mat before me, and make the ground seem alive again. As I stood there, marveling at the changes that would take place, my son came up to share in the moment.

"Look at that, son. What do you think?"

"I think it stinks that B.B. would let that ratty old brown carpet fall out of his truck on the way to the dump, and expect us to pick it up. You oughta talk to the guy."

Break-up has arrived when life takes on a whole new perspective. It offers an opportunity for everyone, no matter where their house might be, to experience the thrill of living on the water's edge. Break-up is here when daily checks are made for salmon swimming up the driveway.

Deep reflection is a sure sign of break-up. Each person is forced to look beyond the surface for a positive identity. This is no more apparent than when leaving the grocery store, and standing in the parking lot.

"Whadaya mean, 'the muddy brown car,' mister? They're all muddy brown."

"Hey! Gimme a break, all right? I'm looking, I'm looking."

Ultimate truths and questions into your own morality come forward as confirmations of break-up. Looking out the window at the banks of retreating snow, deep insights to the truth come forward in the form of yellow and orange bumps. Contrary to what you've been telling the collections people, the paper has actually been delivered through the winter. Should you pay the bill?

Yes, when April and break-up arrive, Alaskans realize the promise of life, and harbor only one thought: hurry up May.

Nailwhackers

Every year, natural phenomena occur to herald the arrival of spring. In San Juan Capistrano, the swallows return to their nests. In Hinckley, Ohio, the buzzards return to their roosts (I have never been to Hinckley, but would suppose it looks real festive with all those brightly colored buzzards). Here on the Kenai Peninsula, many would argue that the snow geese mark spring. In fact, they are just a precursor to the event that genuinely marks the start of spring: the emergence of the purple thumbed nailwhacker.

Unlike the swallows and buzzards, nailwhackers winter over in their habitat. They pass the winter like eagles, sitting glumly, waiting for the opportunity to scarf up some choice tidbit. Patience and persistence pays off when they can swoop in and grab a new hammer here or power saw there. All in preparation for the grand spring emergence.

As the final vestiges of winter's grasp melt away, the nailwhackers stumble out into the bright sunshine, in full toolbelt plumage, eager to send the glorious sounds of "Whack! Whack! Thump, ouch!" echoing through the spring air.

It seems to me that at least eighty percent of the men I know on the Peninsula are purple thumbed nailwhackers. It is a kind of Alaskan rite of passage for a man to build a home or undertake some large modification and/or addition to an existing home. The reasons for this compulsion are many.

First, it is a traditional thing to do. The homesteaders built their homes. After all, we live in "The Last Frontier" don't we? It says so right on our license plates. (We should have kept "North to the Future"). Okay, so that makes it an obligation, not an option.

You'll never hear tales about homesteaders and early residents like "Moose Meat" John calling a construction company to contract the construction of a log cabin or cache. No, by golly, a real Alaskan man builds his own home. Unfortunately, gone are the days of the simple, square log cabin. The early residents in Alaska had a lot more to worry about than having a showplace home with all the creature comforts available. Their main worry was simple: basic survival.

Modern life, though perhaps more complicated, offers more time for elaborate construction.

"So Bert, how's the house coming?"

"Not bad. Last fall, just before I knocked off for the season, I got the third floor on. Even put the Jacuzzi in. But during the winter, I decided it'd be better to have the Jacuzzi in the basement."

"So, whatcha gonna do?"

"Well, I figure to jack the house up, and dig out a basement this summer and..."

Another reason for all the homeowner construction is cost. Everyone thinks they need an extra room just to store all the money they will save by building things themselves. Granted, with your own labor all you pay for is materials, but the bottom line that says "Grand Total" is the one that counts. If an honest job of accounting is performed, figuring in the materials lost to first attempts, and the additional costs incurred from minor incidentals such as stitches, bandages, tetanus shots, and liniment, breaking even against the high bid is the best one can truly hope for.

The existence of all sorts of wonderful tools generates a good deal of the construction that goes on. A real purple thumbed nailwhacker always needs one more tool. It's obvious when a new Sears tool catalogue hits the post office. Men by the score rush out the door with their catalogues clenched tightly in their fists, panting in the eager, glassy-eyed, anticipation of getting home and finding some new, as yet unpurchased, tool. This is because nailwhackers, as a rule, suffer from reverse logic. They don't think, "I have a project, what tool would be best?" No, they think, "Be still, my pounding heart. Here's a tool I don't have! What can I possibly build with it?" *Viola*! Birth of a project.

Women's magazines frequently take the burden of project ideas off the man's shoulders and get spouses into the act. Many opportunities for the nailwhacker to show his stuff are instigated this way: "Hon, I saw a picture of the most beautiful solarium in this month's *House Improbable*. Wouldn't it be nice to have something like that off our bedroom?"

The man sets his Sears tool catalog down thoughtfully and says, "I guess, but our bedroom is upstairs."

"I know, but you could knock out the walls on both floors and build a room under the solarium."

The nailwhacker's expression changes to a dreamy, far away look as his eyes become vacant, focusing on the possibility. "Yeah, we could use another den, in case the other two fill up."

One of the great things about being a purple thumbed nailwhacker is that no experience is needed. No matter what, or how large the project is, somebody is going to tell you how to do it. More often than not, your adviser has become a veritable encyclopedia by watching his neighbors. "Oh yeah, sure. It's no problem putting on a gambrel roof, I watched the guy down my road do his. You'll really save money if you build the trusses your-self. You oughta put shake shingles on it. Looks better with shake shingles."

Of course, once the actual work begins, the adviser is not to be found. Obviously, having already observed a project like yours before, he feels that it's noncompulsory to attend a refresher course. This is why there are so many owner-built homes with no siding. Has anyone actually seen someone put siding on? Or does siding grow out of aged plywood? It's been two years, and my plywood still shows no signs of growth. Maybe I'll give it a few more years.

In the mean time, Sears has a really spiffy moulder/planer on sale. Can you imagine all the fancy window panes that would be possible for use in building a really big greenhouse?

Clamming Up

Let's be up front about this: I don't like clams. That isn't to say that I don't like to eat foods that contain clams-- I do. There isn't anything I'd rather scoop with a chip than clam dip, and clam chowder-- that delectable concoction that would just be potato soup without the little rubbery chunks in it-- is a favorite. I just don't like clams on a personal level, one that involves procuring them.

Clamming is what desperate people that have grown tired of not catching fish do to win bragging rights over some form of aquatic life. This decidedly biased, and perhaps jaded, view is the result of my first and last clamming adventure.

I should have known something was not right the first time I heard the term "clam tide."

"There's a really good clam tide coming up this weekend, you want to go get some?"

Having spent my youth in New Mexico, and other landlocked parts of the country, the vision that came to mind was a flood of water that would leave the beach strewn with little mollusks. This was a pleasant vision, one of just calmly strolling down the beach, a fresh, salty breeze in my face, stooping every now and then to pick up a particularly good looking clam. What a pleasant way to spend an afternoon. Blissfully ignorant of the work involved with the harvesting of clams, I accepted the invitation.

The first thing I learned upon arrival at the beach is what the phrase "good clam tide" meant. I was somewhat dismayed and disappointed that it does not, in fact, mean that the clams will be washed up for your ease in selection. What it means is that most of the water drains out of the inlet to leave vast expanses of dirt that must be moved to find the clams.

"Here, you'll need this."

I eyeballed what looked suspiciously like an oversized, bent garden trowel. "Are you sure?"

"Yeah. I'll carry the gun."

"*Gun*? I thought we were after clams, for cryin' out loud. Are they that big?"

"No, no, it's a clam gun."

"As opposed to an elephant gun. I suppose we don't want to waste any meat, right? Make the shot good, B'wana. We don't want to have to track any wounded clams into the kelp."

By the end of the ensuing barrage, it was clear to me that a "gun" to a clammer is a tube that is open on one end, and capped on the other. The capped end has a small hole in it, so the clammer can force the "gun" down into the sand, and extract the plug of soil, and theoretically, the clam. Another intriguing mental picture destroyed by reality.

The second thing I learned was that clams are sneaky critters. Next to snakes, clams have got to be the slinkiest creatures on the face of the planet. Snakes win the top spot by being able to move around quickly without the benefit of any appendages; clams are defaulted to second position only because they cheat by having one foot. They are just as slinky though, because they run (Or would having one foot mean they hop? Stomp?) through sand, mud and gravel at unbelievable speeds.

This became apparent with the first stop out on the beach.

"Wait a minute. Look. Right there. See all those little marks in the sand?"

I squinted my eyes and strained. In a line, stretching down the beach, was a series of little depressions. My heart skipped a beat in anticipation.

"Oooh, we got 'em now, clam tracks! Must have been a whole herd. Which way were they headed? I can't tell. Boy, they've got a helluva stride for just one foot."

At that point, my mentor plunged his clam gun into the sand with a twisting, rocking motion, sealed the hole with his thumb, and with a mighty grunt, pulled a plug out of the beach. He dropped the plug on the beach, and kicked it. He jammed the tube down again, and retrieved a second plug, then flopped on his belly to jam his arm into the hole. "Gotcha!"

He lay there, squirming and thrashing about. For a moment, I was confused as to exactly who had who, until finally, my guide gave up.

"Had it by the neck, but it got away."

"Do you have to choke them all that way?"

It was my turn next. I was lined up on a promising dimple and instructed to use the shovel to scoop the sand from around the clam's hideout. I was doing a pretty fair job too, until the clam got in the way. At that point, it was explained to me that clam shovels were designed by the Marquis de Sade to inflict maximum discomfort on the clammer. They insure a sort of "fair chase" aspect to clamming.

"No, no, no! You can't pry back like that, or you'll crush the clam every time. You've got to lift straight up, and try to twist the shovel at the same time. It takes some practice."

Over the next couple of hours, while my former friend gunned down dozens of clams, I lifted and twisted desperately, retrieving the mangled remains of only a few particularly slow mollusks. When the tide started back in, we headed back to the truck to continue my education.

"Now's when you usually soak your catch in a bucket of water to get some of the grit out." He looked into my bucket. "In your case, I don't think it'd do much good."

Under close tutelage, I began the shell fragment extraction process.

"This is why you don't want to pry back on your shovel... You missed a piece of shell there. If you get 'em whole, you just flush 'em, then hit 'em with hot water, and they open right up."

After picking all the shell pieces off the innards, we were ready to head into the cleaning process.

The cleaning process involves not only peering into the secrets contained in a clam shell, but actually touching the disgusting mess. First, the tough tips of the neck and foot are nipped off. Then the remaining glob is scooped out of the shell, providing any shell is, in fact, remaining. The grit sack-- a polite term for clam guts-- is cut away from the glob. The precision surgical procedure necessary to remove the grit sack doesn't leave much behind on a trophy sized clam. On the pathetic, crushed mini-clams I collected, it left a scraggly little shred of meat that resembled a pale, misshapened O-ring.

"There you go! Your first clam. Whadaya think?"

"I think I've coughed up more appetizing things than this. And with a lot less effort."

It's been sixteen years since that first experience. Every year since, I've been worried sick that my fishing luck will sour enough to force another attempt.

April Fools

Normally, I am not one to seek out the world of academia. Having spent eighteen years of my life in formal education, my opinion is, there are better ways to spend one's time. (My eighth grade teacher was in total agreement with me on that one subject, which is what prompted her to offer me a generous, early retirement package.) However, my eye was captured by a class titled "Fly Fishing" when, in late February, the schedule for the community schools came out. It was, in fact, tempting enough to cause a breach of my promise to Miss Broadbum to, "Never affront the hallowed halls of education again."

After mulling it over carefully for almost fifteen seconds, I assuaged my guilt by rationalizing Miss Broadbum wouldn't even remember the promise. She is no doubt busy in her own retirement, spending her time in the New Mexican desert, pursuing her favorite hobby: sneaking around, scaring rattlesnakes.

Convinced that there would be a virtual land rush crowd vying for seats in the class, I showed up an hour early the first night. Oddly enough, there wasn't a waiting line, and only eight people showed for the class.

The instructor immediately demonstrated his qualifications to teach the class by walking into the room carrying three graphite fly rods, four fancy reels, a well stocked fly tying kit, and an Orvis fishing vest. All without even stumbling. Most fly fishermen at least slip a little on their own drool when around that much quality gear.

The first night's class was on selecting the proper equipment, and interpreting flyfishese. After five years of selecting equipment, it was a true revelation to learn what all those sales people had actually been saying while helping me spend my money. For instance, when a salesman had said, "What you need is a seven weight, weight forward, Air-Cell with six inch drop rate or something similar with a sink tip... probably with a 2X tippet," I should have known I had the wrong sized pole. I don't know why he just didn't tell me I had the wrong pole. Maybe he didn't want to embarrass me.

The second class focused on where fish hide out. I almost skipped this particular session, feeling that, at best, it would be a review. After three decades of fishing, I *know* where the fish are. They will be wherever I am not. I have even worked out a system to fool the fish into thinking that I am not where they are. This is accomplished by leaving hats, coats, lures and, on occasion, entire tackle boxes dangling in the streamside brush while sneaking up and down the water's edge to different locations.

This second class was also full of new insights. The instructor told us that the fish are where one finds them, and most often they can be found where they feed or rest. As if that weren't enough information to digest for one evening, he proceeded to tell us what kinds of water the fish would most likely feed or rest in. The water he described sounded pretty much like the areas I have been hanging my hats, coats and so forth up in while sneaking to other stretches of water. This just goes to prove that fish are smarter than we think. It also explains why the trout or two I've managed to catch prior to the class have had a squinty eyed, myopic, and often, quite confused, look to them.

The third class covered how the fly fisher gets the fish to bite once they are found. I thought the majority of the time would be spent giving us tips on how to keep the salmon eggs on the hook while flinging the line all around. In actual fact, he launched into a lecture about bugs and their private lives that got quite complex. After listening to him go on and on about what bug stage swims where and when, and what lure looks like which bug, someone tried to cut to the chase by asking what he would recommend as the best all around lure. Again, the instructor surprised me, to say the least, when he calmly replied, "Simple: a booger."

Up until that point, I had firmly believed there was little or nothing I wouldn't do to catch fish. The instructor had finally found a line I would not cross. My mind ran wild with two questions: how can you tie something like that to the hook, and can you give us a good second choice?

I was about to pose those questions, when the instructor offered to show us an example of one of his in a purple hue. I'm not sure if it was the collective gasp, or the stunned expressions, but just before the entire class bolted for the door, the instructor wrote on the blackboard "Woolly Bugger." The release of tension in the room was palpable.

That third class was very informative. I learned not only what to offer the fish, but that enunciation is not of paramount importance in fly fishing.

In the fourth and final class, the instructor covered casting. Casting could be considered one of the major obstacles in the pursuit of fly fishing. Most fly fishing neophytes have a tendency to look like Gene Autry experiencing a dangerous trick lariat malfunction. The result of all the whipping and flinging is that the fly fisher becomes festooned with a massive pile of fly line loops, and ends up resembling Rod Stewart on a bad hair day.

My years of self instruction should have paid off handsomely, but once more, the instructor was a few steps ahead of me. Actually, most of the differences between his casts and mine were semantic in nature.

The instruction started out with the basic "false" cast. The instructor's description roughly fit my own: work the line, but don't land the fly on the water. I had been false casting for years, but the instructor's idea was to keep the fly moving, instead of parked solidly in nearby tree limbs.

Another cast I was already familiar with was the "drop" cast. My drop casting has been subject of numerous discussions.

"How'd you do today?"

"Pretty good. I had a couple of drop casts, but since I was in shallow water, managed to recover the pole both times."

The semantics thing was worked out by the end of the class, and everyone became proficient enough to nail any trout that might have been cruising through the junior high gym.

So here I am, a competent graduate of the community schools course on fly fishing, fully versed in the artful application of simulated arthropods. Unfortunately, the ice isn't going anywhere for the next month and a half. Don't I feel like a victim of a cruel April Fool's joke?

The Spring Smokehouse

Early May is a wonderful time. The days are frequently sunny and pleasant, with just enough chill in the air to keep a jacket nearby in case the wind picks up. Most of the snow is gone, except for the patches in north facing, shady areas. Each morning begins with a symphony of songs as the returning birds stake their nesting territories. Life has an idyllic quality.

There's smoke on the horizon though, and smoke means danger. My neighbor, "Blizzard" Bob (better known as B.B.) has put his turbocharged Belchflame Spew-master snow thrower up on blocks, and turned his attention to his other task of passion: smoking freezer burned fish.

Fresh smoked fish is one of the things that many people miss during the winter months. Frozen smoked fish is tolerable until shortly after Christmas, when it becomes difficult to tell apart from a burned rawhide chew bone. Canned smoked fish is a passable substitute during the desperation of February munchies, but opening a jar or can simply does not slake the desire for the real thing.

The mind and body ache to open a smokehouse door, and feel the moist smoke as it rolls out to tickle the nose and sting the eyes. Fingers itch to reach into that tangy smoke, touch upon a succulent strip of fish, and gingerly pluck it out to peel the skin off and watch the steam rise into the cool air. The thought of sitting in the warm sun, engulfed in the bittersweet, mingled scents of the smokehouse and budding spruce while taking that first bite of warm, salty, smoked fish is strong enough to send the salivary glands into overdrive. Smokehouses yield ambrosia for the soul and the body. At least they should.

Blizzard Bob's smokehouse sits hardly visible through the budding brush, behind cords of neatly stacked wood, on the back side of his lot across the road. We watch it carefully, waiting for the smoke to issue forth. It's only a matter of time until we'll have to warn the kids again, and keep the dog tied up.

B.B. is going to start smoking any day; he can't wait for the salmon to show up, last year's fish will do. He will rummage through his freezer to find several frozen, slightly mummified salmon. He will then try to reconstitute the flesh by soaking them in one of his "secret" brines. Once the flesh has become gooey enough to allow the bones to protrude, held together only by the crusty, leathery skin, he will throw the whole affair into his smokehouse. Then, after a period of time (determined not so much by flavor as the need to dry the pasty flesh to the skin so that it doesn't slough off upon handling), he will prowl through the neighborhood forcing a taste on anyone he can bushwhack.

Declining tactfully doesn't work. More quickly than you can gag, a sample is shoved into your face.

"Hi there! I just finished a batch of fish, try some."

"No, really B.B., I just finished... mmmffff orgk."

"Some of the best I've ever smoked up, huh?"

"Ferbin goncha gorrible phthat."

"Yeah, Knucks said pretty much the same. Well, here's a few pounds for your family. I'm gonna go work on a new brine I've come up with. Man, I nailed 'em last year. Catch ya later."

Less than tactful refusals don't work either. My father-in-law, Joe, was visiting one time when B.B. cornered him. Joe doesn't mince words. When B.B. stuffed a piece of fish in Joe's mouth, Joe spun his head and spit it out so forcefully that his false teeth followed. As we stood there in shock, Joe roared through his gums, "Tha' thlop ith tho bad my tongue bea' my teethp out trying to get away! Whachoo thmoke it withp? *Kapok?*"

"Well, no. I tried an old frontier technique. But we don't have any buffalo around here and... so I ah... moose nuggets. Too much salt?"

It hasn't always been quite so bad. It used to be that just a few fish made it through the winter, and those could be disposed of quickly, by running them through a small electric smoker. All that changed in 1987, the year of "The Big Run." B.B. has never been much of a producer with a rod and reel, but he is extremely proficient with a dipnet. Like many other people, he went out and bought a thirty-one cubic foot freezer to store his catch. With no constraints due to limited storage, B.B. runs amuck in late July.

His neighbors pay the price in the spring.

Since 1987 he has run the gamut of smokers, progressing from the Little Chief to the Webber, continuing right on up, until a genuine smokehouse had to be built. The first actual smokehouse was lost to a mysterious fire last year. One night, the peace and quiet of the neighborhood was shattered by the frantic screams of "Fire! Fire! My smokehouse is burning up!"

Several of us ran over and did the only thing we could. We beat the flames out with axes. We had to work fast. B.B. almost had enough garden hose hooked up to reach the scene. After the last traces of any combustible material were pounded into the dirt, we expressed our sympathy to Blizzard Bob and left him to contemplate how best to rebuild.

We should have invited him to join us in our celebration of a job well done. Maybe we could have convinced him it was all for the best, and it was time to move on to some other springtime diversion. Maybe, but as it is, a new smokehouse appeared over the course of the summer. This one is fireproof. It is built on a cement slab, with two layers of cinder block liner to protect the lower portion of the walls. There will be no errant embers to help us now.

Well Done

Memorial Day is important because, in addition to being a national holiday, it serves as the official start of the barbeque season in Alaska.

Barbequing is important because, in addition to providing some excellent table fare, it remains one of the last unprotested arenas of male dominance. Women, with few exceptions, don't barbeque. It's hard to imagine even the most militant feminist standing up and demanding equal time in the smoke and fumes of the barbequing world. It's not a matter of skill, it's a matter of desire.

There is something about fire that appeals to a man's basal instincts. Even after fifty thousand years, men still succumb to the lure of controlling heat and flame. Like moths, men are drawn to a fire. *Any* fire.

If there is a fireplace, the men will all congregate around it to poke and prod the coals, maybe throw on an extra cord or two, "just to keep it going." Camping is when men are at their peak in fire tending; an open pit is an invitation of unlimited capacity. All the guides for camping indicate a fire pit should be ringed with rocks. This procedural dictum is generally accepted as a means of containing the coals, but actually it serves to limit how much wood is piled up at one time. Barbequing is just a way to fool around with a campfire at home.

As with many of the simpler joys in life, barbequing has been assailed recently by those members of the "faster is better" crowd. There are now two options in barbequing: the standard, old fashioned charcoal method, and the "do it *now*" propane grills. The big difference between the two is the amount of skill involved.

In using the charcoal grill, a general finesse and modicum of ability (not to mention speed) is required to stack the charcoal, douse it with lighter fluid, and escape with your eyebrows intact upon ignition. With the modern, electro-lite propane grill, almost any oaf can incinerate the main course with the simple press of a button.

I say "*almost* any oaf" because of last year's Memorial Day barbeque at Blizzard Bob's.

His annual Memorial Day barbeque is a tradition in our neighborhood. Every year, while half the free world descends upon the lower Kenai Peninsula to fish the early runs of king salmon in the rivers, we spend a relaxing afternoon in the sanctity of our own neighborhood watching B.B. incinerate cow flesh.

The food has never been the major attraction to this affair, as the main course at the Memorial Day barbeque is never worth eating. The draw is the free entertainment.

Just like any neighborhood barbeque anywhere, we have the one fellow that gets tiddly on a few beers and instantly becomes an expert on cooking over flames. Knucks Mahoneigh professes such expertise every year. It seems that his secret to the perfect grilled roast is to pour a little beer over it. This instant marinade serves only to quench the coals and light up B.B.'s ire. With the roast half done, B.B. has to dump the soggy coals, and relight another fire to finish the job. The second half of the cooking is always hurried, and the results are always scorched. If it weren't for all this entertainment, the whole first summer barbeque thing could be shortened by simply serving charcoal briquettes with potato salad.

In an attempt to make the first barbeque as good as the late subsequent ones, B.B. bought a propane grill. His reasoning was simple: "If you can control the heat, there is no chance of burning up the food."

The purchase of his new Sparko-matic Infinite Control Kabob Master came as quite a shock, since B.B. is a fire fusser extraordinaire. He has turned the necessary chore of manipulating coals into a fine art. It was B.B. that first developed the now famous "smiley face" coal pattern, where the coals are arranged in a "smiley face" in the bottom of the grill. This technique places most of the heat to the front of the grill for cooking, and leaves the coals in back for keeping things warm.

I quizzed him about his new grill. "But what about the coals? What will you do for the total experience? Working the coals is most of the pleasure in barbequing."

"No problem. In a propane grill, the bottom is lined with lava rocks. I'll just poke them around a little with the fork now and then. Besides, you know what the best advantage to a propane grill is? It's Knucks-proof. He can dump all the beer he wants, and with a simple press of a button, we'll be back in business."

When we all gathered for the big event, B.B. proudly wheeled out his new grill. There were the obligatory whistles and words of praise. B.B. was in a good humor, and ready to tempt fate.

"Knucks, my good friend! Have a beer! Heck, have two, they're small."

Since there wasn't any real prep time with the Sparko-matic, all the men stood around admiring the new grill while B.B. launched into a monologue about all its marvelous features. He only stopped long enough to offer Knucks another beer now and then.

Finally, it was time to show what the Sparko-matic could do. With a flip of the wrist, and a mash of a thumb, B.B. was ready to cook. He stepped back and eyeballed the heat waves rising from the grill, poked a few lava rocks for good measure, threw on the roast, and laid in wait for Knucks.

Within minutes of the first sputterings from the grill, Knucks was over to lend his advice.

"Fire okay there, bud? Sounds a little hot."

B.B. had been waiting. "Might be. We'll turn the heat down some."

"What kind of seasoning did you use?"

"Nothing. Why?" B.B. knew that Knucks was his.

"*Nothing?* Not even a marinade? That's no good. We'll fix that right now."

B.B. stepped aside, and let Knucks open the grill and douse the roast liberally with a beer. What's more, he stood there and smiled.

As the steam billowed from the heated lava rocks, B.B. calmly lowered the lid, and pressed the ignitor button. Nothing happened. He adjusted the knobs to the "cremate" position, and pressed the ignitor button. Nothing happened.

Knucks, continuing his official barbeque kibitzer role, suggested that B.B. open the lid a little to let the steam out.

B.B. opened the lid part way, and pressed the ignitor.

At the sound of the *ka-whump*, the air was filled with smoking lava rocks. The roast sailed a full four feet into the air. The Sparko-matic Infinite Control Kabob Master separated into two distinct pieces: the lid, which dangled from the end of B.B.'s arm as he stood in total shock, and the body which lay on its side in a smoldering heap.

All present were frozen in surprise. The first to recover from the stunning display was Knuck's dog, Grrr. He jumped up, snatched the roast, and disappeared into the woods.

Three things were learned at last year's Memorial Day barbeque. First, propane grills can, indeed, keep your roast from burning, particularly if it comes off the grill quick enough. Second, peanut butter and jelly goes well with potato salad. Third, there's safety in numbers; nobody packs a propane grill while fishing on the river.

Visiting the Great Land

With the arrival of Memorial Day Weekend, summer is here, and it's time to worry about those annoying pests. As perennial as fireweed, they come to drain you until there is nothing left but a dry husk with a nervous twitch.

Mosquitoes? No, it's the Visitors From Hell. Most Peninsulites of more than three year's residence have had to endure at least one such visitation. Unexpected and/or unwanted guests in the summer are just one of the things that go along with living in an area like ours. It is similar to the risks of contracting malaria while living in tropical areas-- except that malaria is relatively benign in comparison.

A person's sordid past can come back to haunt them in the form of Visitors From Hell. As a child, I never fully understood what might be in store all those times I tormented my sister into screaming mass. Mom swore that someday I'd be sorry. I understand now.

Answering the phone one evening, mumbling about the weekly solicitation for *Time/Life Books*, a cheery, unfamiliar voice began a series of events almost too bizarre and ghastly to comprehend.

"Howdy! You don't know me. I'm Dwayne-Bubba Garsnout. Your sister, Kathy, said that if me, Hildegaard an' the kids ever got to Alaska, you'd be plum tickled to show us around for a few days."

I couldn't remember my sister ever mentioning a Garsnout family, but the rules of Alaskan hospitality dictate a cordiality in greeting even strangers. Sometimes visiting with people that know your family serves as a substitute for actual visits from family. Therefore, hospitality is extended to any visitor that is a friend of family down south. With the element of surprise on the invading force's side, and the pressure on my side to live up to the Alaskan hospitality standards, Dwayne-Bubba soon had directions to our home.

In short order, a large motorhome with a large sign attached to the front that said "Rent Me - *Cheap!*" pulled into the drive.

Hildegaard and Dwayne-Bubba Garsnout along with their progeny and their little dog, Piddles, boiled out of the road whale as soon as it beached itself in the driveway.

Introductions and handshaking were in order. After an hour or two of stimulating discussion about the poor roads in Alaska, how a fortune can be made with Amway, and how a different color scheme would enhance our interior decorating, it was time for bed.

Sleeping arrangements shouldn't have been a problem. After all, our guests had the rented camper. Unfortunately, Dwayne-Bubba had a different idea.

"Ya know, it's sorta crowded with all six of us in there. The kids wouldn't mind sleeping on the floor in the house at all. Would you kids? Piddles usually sleeps with Little Hildey. Good night."

Surveying our charges, I decided they were as delightful as any raised in the deepest jungles by large primates. There was the oldest: an adolescent that thought everything was "lame" unless it could be consumed or turned up to a volume that drew blood. The next in line was the fifth grader: almost translucent from over-exposure to CRT radiation. Nothing was important to this child unless it glowed, beeped, blinked, whirred and played the same rinky-tinky song to distraction. The preschooler was the "curious" child. How many times can the cat flip in the air and still land on its feet? How much smoked salmon will Piddles eat before he throws up... again?

Being from the Lower 48, the kids weren't used to daylight at bedtime. The adolescent wasn't problem, just feed his tape player a four course meal of batteries, and he'd rock himself to sleep. The vidiot could be dealt with by locating him near an electrical outlet, so he can work on his pallor until sleepy. The pre-schooler was a problem. Actually, bears were the problem, and Little Hildey knew it.

"Daddy says bears will get me if I'm bad. And I made Piddles throw up."

"Oh, that's not really bad," I assured her, "it's not good mind you, 'cause we're out of carpet cleaner. Bad would be if you were to, say for instance... strangle a family of five and their dog for dropping in uninvited. Besides, you have Piddles to protect you. By the way, does Piddles need to go outside?"

"What for?"

With the kids settled in downstairs, and the adults hiding in the motorhome, it was time to escape and slip into the comforting nonexistence of sleep. As I floated off, dreaming of living in an area where the roads don't go, the stillness of the night was rudely shattered.

"*BEAR!* It's a Bear! It's gonna get me!"

Piddles was in full yap as we stumbled down the stairs into bedlam. Little Hildey, backed against the far wall, pointed at the ground level window. The fifth grader was thrashing about, caught in his sleeping bag where he had managed to garrote himself with his video game power cord. The adolescent was oblivious to the commotion, thinking it was a refrain from his latest cassette. A large, black shape peered in from outside the window. Butcher the wonder dog, had returned from his latest roll in a nearby pile of fish guts.

Reassurance was needed in this situation, so we let Butcher inside to show how harmless he really is. Little Hildey's screams became one, long, high-pitched wail. Piddles' yapping doubled in volume and climbed two octaves. The little ball of noisy fur made two laps around Butcher and then fell over on his side. The room suddenly became deathly quiet. Butcher decided he was obviously at the wrong house, and exited just as Dwayne-Bubba burst onto the scene.

"What in blazes is all the commotion? And what the hell is that *stink*?"

Little Hildey immediately runs to Daddy and sets the record straight, "They let a bear in to get me, and it killed Piddles!"

Little Hildey's accusation was the perfect cue for Hildegaard's entrance. With hysterics about to reach a fevered pitch, the children were ushered upstairs, so the adults could hash out the situation.

Upon examination, it became apparent that at least the last part of Little Hildey's claim was true. Piddles was, in fact, quite dead. Hildegaard and Dwayne-Bubba were devastated.

In an effort to be tactful and sympathetic, I offered a choice of actions. "Would you like me to bury him out back? Or there's a dummm... a borough sanitation depository just down the road."

"No!" Hildegaard was vehement. "I won't leave poor Piddles in this Godforsaken wilderness. We'll take him home for burial."

Dwayne-Bubba stepped in to take charge, "Hildegaard's right. We're leavin' in the morning. We have arrangements to make. The vacation's ruined. We'll drive back to Anchorage tomorrow."

In respect for the bereaved, we offered absolutely no argument. The deceased was prepared for travel by wrapping him in a plastic bag and placing him gently in the chest freezer. The following morning an ice cooler would be gladly donated for the trip home. The Garsnouts retired as a family to their camper to console one another.

The next morning there was tension in the air. As the kids and the cooler/casket were loaded, I tried to smoothe things over with Dwayne-Bubba. He obviously held me personally responsible for Piddles' demise. I tried touching on the one thing we had in common: my sister, who started the whole unfortunate mess.

"Say hi to Kathy for me when you get back to Burney."

"Burney?"

"Yeah, where my sister and you live."

"We don't live in Burney."

"Oh, really? You've moved then."

"No, never lived in Burney. I met your sister when she came to San Francisco to buy a used car."

"Ahhh... I see. In that case, I'll give her *your* regards when I call her tonight."

As bad as a visit from non-relatives may be, the absolute worst case visitor from hell scenario is the family reunion.

Family reunions exist to remind us of why we left home in the first place. They also open a veritable floodgate of visitors that can plague a household for the entire summer.

Most family reunions held on the Peninsula begin without the knowledge of the hosting home. They usually start out as an honest desire on Mom and Dad's part to see the grandchildren.

"Hubert, wouldn't it be nice to see the grandkids and visit Katy and what's-his-name?"

"Sure would. I'll bet we'd hardly recognize Joey and Amanda. Say, wouldn't it be great for all the kids and grandkids to get together? Have a regular reunion."

"Oh Hubert! Let's call them right now and set it all up."

"Katy and ol' what's-his-name?"

"No. Joe and Cheryl, Tillie and Bob, and Pete and Connie."

Generally, all invited parties are gung-ho on the idea of a reunion in Alaska. Since Mom and Dad seem set on the crazy idea of having a reunion somewhere, they all want to make sure it's as far from their own homes as possible. Unfortunately, it never fails that someone wants to arrive a little before the big event, and others want to stay a little after the termination of hostilities.

Everyone wants the opportunity to have the hosts to themselves. This stretches the invasion out for a period of weeks instead of just days. The end result is similar to the sacking and occupation of Rome. However, I believe the Vandals at least provided their own beer.

Once the plans for maximum impact are made, and everyone has their tickets, the unwitting hosts are clued in on the impending assault.

A bright and cheerful, "Hey! Guess what?" is a sure give away that the next words spoken will be, "We're coming up for a visit."

"Not at the peak of the red salmon run! Er... I mean, how nice. When?"

"Well, Mom an' me won't get there until the last week of July, but Joe and Cheryl will be there the nineteenth, and Tillie and Bob will get there five days after us, with Pete and Connie getting there the third of August. So we can have the reunion on..."

"Wait a minute! Wait a minute! All this great news is a little tough to handle in one, long breath. Reunion? The *entire* family is coming?"

"Wouldn't be a reunion without the whole family. Besides, we got a deal on the tickets, but we can't make any changes to 'em."

It is not possible to convince me that the airline companies aren't in cahoots with my relatives down south. This bit about "no refund" tickets was undoubtedly my in-laws' idea.

The middle of July arrives, and so do Joe, Cheryl, and their kids. Their luggage does not.

Joe is really excited to see us. "Oh man, I'm glad you were waiting for us, let's go. My team plays on ESPN at five."

"Gee, Joe, we don't have cable at the house."

"Get real! This is part of the United States. Right?"

By the end of the week, Joe has provided in-depth, play-by-play accounts of every great ball game he has ever witnessed, Cheryl has provided seven wonderful examples of her wok cooking skills, and their luggage is still on the loose. Not a problem for Cheryl and the kids, plenty of clothes their size around the homestead. Not so with the Joe. The big guy is getting a bit gamey.

Mom and Dad's arrival will at least provide a little diversion from Joe's running sports recollections. Pulling into the driveway, the radio fishing report indicates a near-record run of red salmon are about to hit the river.

Hubert comments, "Well! I'd say we got here just in time."

Feeling a faint glimmer of hope I ask, "How so?"

"You've really let the yard slip since my last visit. We've got our work cut out for us."

The next five days are spent in forced labor around the yard. Fortunately, friends are kind enough to call nightly to keep me abreast of the phenomenal fishing I'm missing.

Tillie and Bob arrive ahead of schedule and are found staring at the trophy mounts in the terminal. Cordial greetings are cut short to express their shock and disgust with the crass and vulgar display of "wantonly slaughtered animal life."

I decide that perhaps it would be better to let Cheryl fire up the old wok again instead of barbecuing the home made caribou sausage to celebrate their arrival.

There is good news. Joe and Cheryl's luggage finally made it. Everyone can breathe a little easier.

Pete and Connie step off the plane, on August third, sporting their finest Patagonia safari wear. Pete's ensemble is completed with his matching patent leather hiking boots and cellular phone holster. Connie looks smashing in her fluorescent green fleece jacket, tan twill pants and black nylon hiking boots. Live, from Los Angeles, the new age pioneers have arrived to conquer the Last Frontier.

The evening of the third brings a cool wind with rain right behind. On the fourth, the drizzle is broken only intermit-tently by raging downpours. The family members are more than just symbolically close as they all huddle under the carport for the reunion.

Tillie and Cheryl are swapping wok/vegetarian recipes. The other ladies are alternating stints at riding herd over the kids and stirring potato salad.

All the other men are in a heated filibuster over a myriad of subjects ranging from baseball to bluechip stocks to lawn care. As I stand over the barbecue, watching Tillie and Bob's soy-burgers squirm through the grill, Hubert walks up.

"This is great. We oughta do this every year."

"Yeah, sounds fun. I hope you all enjoy it, but we won't be able to join you next year."

Hubert is surprised. "Why not?"

"We'll be using our super-advanced, non-refundable tickets for Australia next summer."

However, a determined Alaskan resident doesn't necessarily have to endure endless unwanted visitors. There are ways to defend one's home.

Since a phone call is usually the harbinger that blazes the trail for the unwanted visitors, it only follows that a good telephonic defense system will cut down the traffic significantly.

One could simply keep the phone off the hook, but there are disadvantages to this system. Legitimate calls need to get through, and sooner or later someone will forget to maintain the defense, and hang up the phone when done using it. Even such a minor breach can result in an all-out invasion.

Some folks reading this are sitting there smugly confident in their telephone answering machine's ability to shield them from harm. Answering machines are good for short-term barrage assaults like calls from work, or pesky neighbors, but they just won't perform reliably as a defensive tool in the long siege of summer visitors. Ultimately, the answering machine serves as nothing more than an early warning device. After a few messages requesting that you call back, Aunt Myrtle will simply state her arrival date.

A better alternative is the disguised defense system. This method of discouraging the influx of visitors is simple: always answer your phone with a foreign accent. The less intelligible, the better.

"Da, who is speakink?"

"Hello, this is Aunt Myrtle."

"Mortle is not beink here."

"No, no, I am Myrtle. Where are Bill and Joan?"

"They are beink not here also. Thankink you, goodbye."

This sort of defense doesn't cost anything, as Aunt Myrtle will call the operator to report a wrong number, get credit, and call back.

"Is beink good day."

"You again! For Pete's sake."

"He is not beink here vith Mortle or Bill and Joan. You are hafink numbers beink bad. Da? Good-bye."

If Myrtle is really determined, she might call back a third time, but frustration and embarrassment in reporting yet another wrong number will hedge any bet against it. One of the additional benefits of the disguise defense is that after a conversation or two, even the salespeople from *Time/Life Books* and *Hunting and Fishing News* will quit calling.

No defense is foolproof. A really sneaky relative might call in the middle of the night, catching you unawares, so the phone is answered without the foreign accent. Or it could be that someone recognizes your voice through the accent. In either event, a reliable back-up plan is a necessity. The emergency excuse system is that plan.

Let's take a look at the emergency excuse system in action. Here's the scenario: it's two in the morning, I'm sound asleep, and the phone on the night stand blasts me into semiconciousness. Swinging my feet out of bed and smack onto Butcher the wonder dog's midsection starts a series of reactions that include, but are not limited to wild, high-pitched yelping, loud and startled screaming, falling, lots of thrashing about and answering the phone with a simple, if not somewhat shaken, "Hello?"

"Oh, thank goodness I got through! This is Aunt Myrtle. I'm sorry to call at this odd hour, but I kept getting a wrong number during the day, and end up talking to the rudest foreign sounding person. It must have something to do with sunspots."

Am I caught? Do I panic?

Not on your life, and not at all. I am confident and serene in the knowledge that there is a sheet of paper within arm's reach, posted right along with all the other emergency information. The sheet contains sure-fired, guaranteed to stop 'em dead in their tracks, positively no-visitors-no-way excuses. I simply flip on the light and begin.

"Gosh, Aunt Myrtle, it doesn't look good for this summer. I have a series of bone spur operations scheduled for June and most of July. After that, I'm scheduled for a high-intensity 'Finding Yourself Through Mantra' seminar. And I'm afraid that August is my month to volunteer as lifeguard at the Cook Inlet Mudflats swimming beach. Of course, September is out. That's when all the trophy clammers come up, and I guide. Perhaps some other time..."

Lists should be posted at every phone, and it is a good idea to have the kids get comfortable with the procedure. I make unannounced test calls throughout the months when visitors are a real threat, and critique the kids' performance.

Good defenses will stem the flow of most visitors, but a few will get through. It is important to know what to do with those that do.

The first thing to remember is that real life is on your side. The Department of Tourism spends massive amounts of money to lure visitors up here with television ads. Alaskans don't normally see them, not just because they aren't a target audience, but because the state doesn't want to get sued when an Alaskan chokes to death in a fit of hysterical laughter.

The ads show merry travelers enjoying the state's grandeur, smiling broadly in a gentle, refreshing breeze, as the warm sunshine brings a brilliant glow to all they survey. Obviously, since the tourism folks have spent only a few million dollars, the camera crews didn't stick around long enough to actually capture the sun. The ads are produced with trick photography and the use of mirrors.

If, by some freak weather system, it should happen that the sun does shine, it's important not to start running around, showing the visitor a good time. Remember: word-of-mouth advertising has built and destroyed empires. Send back one disgruntled visitor, and ten future incursions will be prevented.

There are ways to insure that a visitor's experience is less than ideal, thereby preventing repeat visits and potentially shortening the current one.

An effective method is to let Mother Nature do the work. Mosquitoes can be immensely helpful when it comes to dissuading larger pests. Before heading out to explore the wilderness of Alaska, I get two bottles of lotion type repellent. I empty one, and replace the contents with an unscented hand lotion. This will becomes the visitor's personal bottle of repellent, and my ticket to freedom.

Another means in which visitors can be encouraged to seek alternate sites for spending their leisure time is to maintain an extensive library devoted to bear attacks. Several different books covering the subject in gruesome detail are kept laying about our home. We always put one on the coffee table, and set another right on the visitor's night stand. One might even want to go so far as to actually sit and read one or two particularly graphic passages out loud. This generally sets the thought processes in motion about perhaps checking out other places to visit. Especially when you follow up the stories with comments about fishing or camping in areas "as wild and free as the ones in that book by your bed."

Additionally, there is always some sort of useful outdoor activity that a visitor can help out with if the sun happens to shine. Laying in firewood immediately comes to mind. What a truly Alaskan experience. With the help of the visitor it's possible to cut, split and stack at least four cords in a week. It doesn't matter that we heat with gas, we can sell the wood come fall, and the visitor will go back with a genuine Alaskan experience and resolute determination not to return.

Other possibilities include finishing building projects. One year, a plumber visited us, and left behind a new bathroom. After the bathroom was finished, I took him fishing. The fishing was done in typical weather, except the wind was blowing hard enough to keep the waves flatter than usual. That was five years ago. It's fortunate that we haven't needed any plumbing work since.

Even with a good rate of dodging and dissuasion, there will be visitors. There will also be visitor burnout. Visitor burnout can

136

prove to be a serious affliction. One year, after back to back visits from my parents, a niece and nephew, and two brothers, my wife came down with a nasty case of stress induced hives.

What Alaskans need is a good counseling system of support groups for visitor victims. It could be staffed by volunteers, people that have been through the wringer of over visitation themselves. Open discussions on coping techniques could be offered. Previous stressed-out hosts could share what they have learned. Specialists that deal in traumatic events, such as hostage situations, could come and speak. There could be seminars on relaxation techniques and three hundred ways to cook fish gruel. The need is real.

The tough part would be shaking the visitors long enough to obtain the benefits of a support group. However, even that poses no real problem. Almost every community has a visitor's center. One of the rooms at the center could be set aside for "Locals Only," where all the support group's activities could be held. Alaskans could let their visitors wander about the center, while taking in a soothing balm of support.

Additionally, a hot line could be set up. Such a phone system could be a real sanity saver when things got really bad around the old homestead and there was no way to make it into the center. One could simply dial a number for advice. It could even be a toll free number; something catchy and easy to remember, like 1-800-NO GUEST.

It's an idea whose time has come. Now all we have to do is find a program director. The major problem is that the position would be seasonal, and restricted to the summer months. Most of the people I know that would volunteer for the job are too busy showing guests around to fill the position.

The Lawns of Summer

Quick! Name one thing that serves no earthly purpose other than to cause domestic discord, and devour someone's short and valuable time in the summer. If you named lawn beautification, also called "Estate Grounds Enhancement,"
you are correct. (If you named playing golf, you were close, but we're talking primarily about sane people here.)

Over the course of history, it has become unclear as to who came up with the concept of the tended lawn. This comes as no surprise. If you knew for a fact that one of your ancestors was responsible for the development of an idea that has enslaved so many people on their weekends and vacations, would you want it to become public knowledge? No, I suspect that little bit of history is some family's deep, dark secret, a skeleton that they hope never pops out of the closet.

It is even less clear as to why Alaskans spend so much time trying to create beautiful lawns. We are normally such a proud and independent group. What ever happened to the old "I don't care what they do on the Outside" attitude? As soon as the subject of lawns comes up, we fall in line like sheep.

What worsens the situation even further is the fact that most of the lots around here are large. Down South, where folks drool over the thought of a large corner lot of almost a quarter acre, lawn care is not such a big deal.

"Honey, dinner won't be ready for another fifteen minutes, why don't you pop out and mow the front yard?"

"Fifteen minutes? Geez dear, I dunno... maybe I oughta edge the sidewalk too. That'll leave just enough time to shower before we eat."

Here, with the exception of a few Lower Forty-eight look alike subdivisions, if the entire lot is planted in lawn, the send off is a little different.

"I packed your food, dear. And your jacket is in the knapsack in case the weather turns bad. The mosquito repellent is rolled up in your sleeping bag."

"Thanks. Be sure and show the kids my picture now and then so they don't forget me. Bye."

Now, let's throw in the fact that our summers are brief. There is a lot of living to be crammed into that short span of warm weather we call summer. So basically, what we're left with is a situation that requires us to cover more area in less time than our counterparts down south.

Is this fair? I think not, but we have no one to blame but ourselves.

Tended lawns, just like exercise, are the result of the great motivator: guilt. How many Alaskans first moved into their homes with the perfect natural lawn? I'll bet there was just the perfect combination of clump grass, fireweed, and lupine. Probably there was just a touch of highbush cranberries for that musky fall scent. Maybe a little devil's club on the outer edges for the ideal privacy hedge, too.

The men thought, "Oh yeah! Not a tended lawn in sight. I *really like* this neighborhood."

The ladies were thinking, "All we need to do is slash and burn that jungle off the front acreage, spread out about a zillion pounds of grass seed..."

For the first year or two, the natural lawn was safe. Then *they* moved into the home just down the road. You know who *they* are. Every neighborhood eventually gets *them*. Usually they're like this totally radical couple from, you know, like, California. Californians have this, like, awesome and totally uncontrollable urge to like, *cultivate* things. And the next thing you know, the great motivator's little voice is niggling at you, "Doesn't that lawn look nice? Shouldn't we do something about that jungle in front of our home?"

For some strange reason, most men find that the sound of water lapping against the side of a boat seems to shut off the voice of guilt. Women aren't so lucky, and pretty soon the little voice is joined in harmony with a voice that counts. The questions become personal in nature at that point:

"When are you going to make our lawn look that nice? Why don't you do something about that jungle in front of our home?"

Once that point is reached, it will be a long time before another carefree summer is more than merely the stuff of dreams.

It wouldn't be so bad if all a person had to do was cut down and clear the trees, pull all the stumps, slash-rip- tear-scrape all the lower vegetation away, lug off the large rocks, haul-spread-rake-smoothe the top soil, lime-fertilize- seed the whole shebang and occasionally mow the mess. No, that would only take the majority of one, two, possibly at the most, three summers. If it were only that simple!

Once that little layer of delicate green fuzz starts, the real work begins. The balance of nature has been upset, and one pays dearly for such a transgression.

The soil has been tilled and made rich and sweet, so that even something as ill-suited as lawn grass can survive. Hardier, more natural plant species find it an invitation to party down. Eventually the chickweed, dandelions, cottonwood seedlings, and anything else you don't want, is going to show up. Now, on the alternate days that you aren't mowing, you will pluck, pull, pinch, gouge, rip, snip, burn, spray and tear at the invaders. That's the good news. The bad news is that those minor blemishes are of little consequence when compared to an infestation of lawn mange.

Lawn mange is a collection of little dead spots that appear for no reason whatsoever, randomly throughout an otherwise healthy lawn. There is no cure, but therein lies the hope. Placing driftwood strategically on the mangey spots is an excellent way to cover them up and end all your lawn problems at the same time. Since lawn mange appear randomly, it will appear the lawn is being artistically landscaped. With the way the mange spots multiply, in just a few short years, your lawn will look like the high tide mark after a Category IV hurricane.

Utilizing the driftwood approach to lawn care has the added benefit of legitimizing fishing trips.

"Honey, I'm going to go find some more driftwood for the lawn."

"Is that a fact? What's that in your hand?"

"Oh, that... I'm taking the fishing pole to snag some from the the river. The best pieces are on the bottom."

Once the lawn is tightly covered with driftwood, the effect of a random fireweed or two shooting up through the crevices between logs will make a statement: "It's a jungle out there. It's supposed to be."

Rainy Camping

Ask most people what draws them to Alaska, and they will likely respond that it is the outdoor activities. With the fishing, hunting and hiking found right here on the Kenai Peninsula, we live an outdoor enthusiast's dream come true.

Ask most people what it is about the Kenai Peninsula they like least, and chances are good that they will mention rain. Rain and extended outdoor activities are a love/hate combination: people love to do things in the outdoors, and hate to do them in the rain. Unfortunately, waiting for dry weather may result in waiting until the summer is over and all opportunity for doing anything worthwhile has passed.

To go out for the day on a fishing trip or a day hike in the rain is an inconvenience. To camp in a tent overnight, or for several days, in inclement weather is a completely different matter. It's like the difference between having a case of the twenty-four hour flu versus suffering from severe parasitic dysentery.

Tent campers are a persecuted lot. A quick glance around any of the maintained campgrounds in Alaska will quickly demonstrate exactly what I mean. In developed campgrounds, there are two types of sites: those that are designed for motor homes, and those that are intended for tent use. The two types of sites differ in how they are developed.

Camp sites intended for motor homes will have raised, smooth, well tended surfaces in which to park upon. They are carefully engineered to provide a raised surface so that the rain will drain off to prevent the pad from becoming wet and soft. They are usually contoured in such a manner as to drain toward the tent sites.

The average tent site will be arranged so that there is a lumpy, bowl-like depression located at the extreme downhill end of the site in which to set up the sleeping quarters. The bowl-like depression serves as a flood control reservoir to protect any motorhome sites that might be otherwise subject to high water. Sometimes there will be a raised area available in or near the intended tent site that looks promising. After the first stake or two is destroyed, it will be determined the mound is a moss covered pile of rocks or a submerged boulder.

Setting up a tent in the rain is one of life's bigger challenges. This being true because tents are designed and tested by people that don't use them because they don't have to. Camping gear engineers make enough money that they can afford motor homes. Additionally, there is a world of difference between the conditions in which a tent is tested by the manufacturer and the conditions in which it is actually used.

"Say Harry, the shock cords on this model 402B seem a little long... I'm sweating here trying to get the second pin into the grommet... what say you turn the air conditioner up a little?"

"How's that? Say... it's break time. Let's go grab a cup of coffee. It's not like we have to hurry... we're not out in the rain or anything."

"Right. Man! This test floor is killing me. I sure wish they'd have put more pad under the carpet."

In the real world of rain, wet tents become living entities that act like voracious amoebas. Shock cords disappear into their shiny protoplasmic sleeves like food items. Even if the shock cords are successfully forced all the way through the sleeves, the rain soaked top and floor bond in such a manner that they can't be easily separated. The only hope for prying the two halves apart is sending a brave volunteer into the dank and dangerous maw of the tent creature to force the top up. After every rainy weekend, I half expect to see headlines in the paper proclaiming some unfortunate family was devoured by their wet tent.

News item from *The Peninsula Clarion*:

Family Disappears While Camping

Cooper Landing, Alaska-- On Friday, during one of the worst downpours in the Kenai Peninsula's history, a family of four disap-peared while setting up their tent. The only witness to the event was Guy Roap, a tent design engineer from Schenectady, New York, who was camped nearby in his Behemoth Designs motor-home.

"I heard these muffled cries, but didn't pay much attention to them because I was listening to Pavarotti on my stereo. It wasn't until I heard a huge, sloppy belch that I looked outside. I could have sworn I saw what looked like a Model 402B slithering off into the brush."

One of the more cruel jokes that tent engineers have played on the consumer is the invention of the rain fly. It sounds so promising, doesn't it? Too bad putting on the rain fly is the last step to setting up the tent.

"Whatcha got there, Herb?"

"It's a *rain fly*. The last step in putting up the tent is attaching the rain fly."

"Looks neat. What does it do?"

"Well... its purpose is two-fold. First off, it keeps any moisture that got into the tent, prior to adding the rain fly, from escaping, and secondly, it provides the perfect aerodynamic plane for providing enough lift in the lightest of breezes to insure the tent is torn to shreds."

"Wow. Bet the guys in marketing love that."

With the tent properly set up-- that is to say, with the sleeping bags rolled out to absorb all the water puddling in the middle-- it is time for the campers to turn their attention to the other matters. The trials of camping in bad weather are just beginning.

No camping trip would be complete without a campfire. It is a law of nature that campers must burn three times their body weight in fire wood every day just to survive. Rainy weather campfires prove to be a true tribulation in the wet weather camper's survival.

There are two kinds of firewood: available firewood, and suitable firewood. That is why all campground guide books and campground facilities in Alaska list their firewood under camp site amenities as, "firewood: available." Available firewood is what suitable firewood becomes after the rain starts. Available firewood is the mushroom of the fuel world: it just mysteriously appears in wet, cool weather.

"Gee Dear, look what I found... four cords of wood right behind the camp site. I didn't even notice it until the rain started."

Working with available firewood is an exercise fraught with fruitless effort, and a lesson in mental agony. Available firewood doesn't do anything as straightforward as refuse to burn, but it doesn't actually burn with any detectable heat, either.

When working with available firewood, it doesn't matter how carefully the fire is laid, or in what manner, once the tinder is gone, so are the flames. When burning at full heat, the available firewood crackles and pops, sizzles and steams, and then sets into a mode of massive smoke production. This is where the inexperienced lousy weather camper gets into trouble.

"Lookit that fire, Martha! I did it. I got the thing goin'. All it needs now is a little coaxing... I'll just... *whooofwhooof*... hunker down here... *whooofwhooof*... and blow on it a little... *whoofwhoofff*..."

"Bert, get your face outta the mud and ashes. Bert? Bert!"

Bert has become another victim of available firewood hyperventilation.

Fortunately, the modern camper isn't reliant upon the old fashioned campfire for cooking. We have at our disposal a myriad of camp stoves that burn more reliable fuels. Just because they burn and produce heat however, does not mean a meal of any palatability is in the offing.

Cooking in the rain presents unique difficulties. In the interest of keeping the flame on the stove lit, most cooking is done with a large skillet or griddle so the burner plate is protected. This makes preparing things like soup a real challenge. (The whole secret is to use powdered soups. Just sprinkle them on the griddle and stir quickly, letting nature add the water.) During rainy weather, there is no such cooking technique as frying. Alaskans that have experience in wet weather camping have developed a taste for poached bacon with their steamed toast for breakfast.

One of the worst things about camping in the rain is that all your old camping misadventures are brought back to mind. Smells are some of the most powerful triggers for evoking memories, and sleeping bags are the time capsules of the smell world. Damp weather brings out all the old events a sleeping bag may have recorded over time.

"Whooee! What stinks?"

"Hey Dad, remember the time we were camping, and Ol' Butcher rolled in those dead salmon... and then crawled into your sleeping bag?"

"Yeah Dad, and what about the time Jimmy ate that whole pack of hotdogs and a can of chili and got sick... Remember how you couldn't get out of his way?"

There comes a point during the precipitation that it is time to pack up and head home. Even the most ardent camping enthusiasts must pay heed to their survival instincts. Generally, this happens when the entire camp has been flattened by gale force winds and the large trees around the camp have been pummeled into leafless stumps by driving rain.

When the camp looks like an assemblage of flotsam, the most passionate of the family's campers (usually it's Dad) will offer an observation on the weather, "Well, it doesn't look like it's going to get any better. I guess we might want to think about heading home..."

From that instant on, any additional discussion is uttered as a soliloquy. As the rest of the family leaves a frothy, brown wake in their hasty departure, Dad is left behind to pack up camp by himself.

The single advantage to camping in the rain is packing up the camp remnants. Since it will all have to be set out to dry at home, it can be done in a haphazard fashion. The tent is simply balled up and stomped upon to get most of it into the carrying case. A fifty percent recovery on the tent stakes is not simply acceptable, but an enviable achievement. Dishes, cooking gear, and left over food are tossed into the grub box, and the lid is forced closed and latched. When all the loose odds and ends are secreted away into whatever space is available, Dad wades to the car, lugging the last of the gear with him.

The final phase to wet weather camping, the drive home, is the best. As the campers warm up and dry out, good humor returns and the adventure is reflected upon fondly. The drive home also provides time to make the decision on what video movie to rent.

After all, wet weather camping is why the movie rental places stay open late on Friday nights.

Happy Campers

Summer is a time for kids to kick back and relax, that is, until they start whining about being bored. They will start the "I'm bored" routine about the last week in June. That is why there are summer camps for kids. After the initial glow of happiness over not having to attend school has worn off, and the "I've done that" doldrums start to make their presence known, parents need a break from all the summer fun the kids aren't having.

This is nothing new. When I was a kid, my parents would threaten to send my sister to summer camp. Her oscillating whine would barely have drifted away, and the reply would drop like a sack of sand, "Maybe we should send you to summer camp... again."

"No! I'm fine. I have lots to do. I'm going to play now. See ya later."

I was never given an option. Usually the first day out of school for the summer I heard, "You'll be leaving for Alkali Flats Summer Camp tomorrow. Are you packed?"

The next morning, well before dawn to preclude the possibility of neighbors responding to my pleas of help, I would be rustled from bed amid a whirl of assorted clothing, writing materials, dental care products, and towels thrown into the car and dumped at the bus terminal. As the bus pulled out, my folks would smile at me bravely and wave. Just as the bus would turn the corner, they would start jumping up and down while hugging each other.

Things haven't changed much. Basically, there are two kinds of camps for kids: church affiliated and Scout camps. Between the two types, there is really very little difference. They are both run by nonprofit organizations, and the costs are usually reasonable.

I know some parents are out there mumbling that I haven't priced summer camps lately, but actually, a bored child can easily eat the cost of a summer camp tuition in less than a week. A bored child will start with the good stuff, and munch their way through to the things that are good for them until nothing edible is left in the house. At that point, they will be hungry for lunch. (The only exception to this rule is broccoli. The universal children's cry of "Death before broccoli!" assures a constant supply of that particular foodstuff.)

Summer camps all have the same goal in mind: to get the kids out of their parents' hair while providing a good, healthy atmosphere with plenty of wholesome activities that are intended only to maim, not kill.

Somewhere along the line, someone ordained that all summer camps would have to meet certain requirements in order to be a certified operation. The criteria have little or nothing to do with the camp's merit in regards to developing healthy children, the camp simply has to put forth an effort to provide certain amenities and activities to be considered a bona fide summer camp.

One requirement of all summer camps is the operation of a mess hall. The dining that a camp offers can make or break the camp's reputation. In order to qualify as an acceptable mess hall, the cuisine provided has to be "nourishing," and merit no remarks that could possibly be misconstrued as complimentary. You will never see a summer camp brochure bragging on its fine food. Camps are intended for building strong character.

One activity that every camp in the country must offer is canoeing. It matters not where the camp is located, canoeing will be listed among all the fun things campers can try. Even Alkali Flats Camp offered canoeing. Right there in the beautiful white sands of the New Mexican desert, we learned everything one could possibly want to know about portaging canoes.

Alaska has an advantage in the canoe department. Not only is there plenty of water to be had, the water offers an added bonus by way of experience in cold water survival training. Cold water survival training is usually the second thing Alaskan summer camp canoeists learn. The first is that one never stands up in a canoe.

Of course, horses are a must for a real summer camp experience. Those days soaked in soft golden summer light while clinging desperately to the neck of a rampaging, wild-eyed, nag will live in a child's memory forever. Summer camp horses are a different animal altogether from what is normally accepted as a horse. Summer camps become the refuge for horses that are too vicious to be used in the bronc-riding circuits anymore. Most, if not all, seem to have developed a particular fondness for hearing small children wail in unspeakable horror. Many summer camp horses are only casual vegetarians, having discovered that an occasional camper makes a tasty break in the normally bland diet of oats and grass. Those that don't bite on a regular basis, kick with uncanny accuracy.

Another must in the activities department is archery. No summer camp worth its tuition is without an archery program. This is the singularly most popular activity kids can look forward to. After an entire year of hearing Mom warn, "Be careful with that stick, you'll poke someone's eye out!" campers are handed a bundle of sharp, pointy sticks, and the means to propel them long distances. Summer camps with intensive archery programs discourage families from sending siblings at the same time because of the "Tell Law." The law is simple: any combination of siblings, mixed with a bow and arrow will eventually result in a reenactment of the William Tell legend.

One of the important aspects of summer camp for kids is the opportunity for them to learn a little more about the natural world they live in, and their place in it. A program on animal lore is a must for a quality camp. Not only is the program a summer camp industry standard, the class is pretty much standard, albeit short. The programs all address the subject of bears.

"If you wander around at night here, the bears will get you, so don't make trouble."

This teaches the children their position in the natural world: the bottom of the bear's food chain. Although it helps the camp counselors maintain curfew, and provide quality party time, it can cause dehydration among the campers. One casual remark by a counselor mentioning bear activity at night will ensure that all liquid consumption will stop shortly after lunch. Who wants to make that long, lonely, dangerous trip to the outhouse after dark?

Fortunately, the human body can survive with limited water for well over a week, which is why most summer camps are about one week long. At the end of that week, parents find their returned campers different people. They are happy to just sit around the house quietly. Whining about being bored doesn't seem so important after staring into the maw of death for five to seven days. At least not until next summer.

Camping History

Above my dresser is a large photograph of a young man paddling a canoe on a quiet river. On the matting is a hand written inscription, "Lawrence W. Kinne, mouth of the Platte River, 1915." The young man in the picture is my grandfather. The river is a small thing, located in Michigan. Grandpa was camping when the picture was taken.

Camping was simply part of the daily grind, merely the hotel/motel of getting somewhere, to our forefathers. Lewis and Clark were big on camping. Camping is in Americans' blood.

We are lucky here on the Kenai Peninsula. Every summer we not only can readily partake in camping, but can also observe how it evolved into what it is today. The secret in truly appreciating camping is being able to view the current situation and compare it to the experiences of our forefathers. Remember, history really does repeat itself, it just looks a little different.

Traditionalist campers are those folks that envision them-selves in the picture of Lewis and Clark that everyone who has ever endured a class in American history has seen. We all know the one. In the picture, the subjects are standing on a ridge, looking mighty sharp in their buckskins and packs, as Sacajawea points off into the horizon to the next campsite. With the addition of a few bright changes in the color scheme, that could be any group of R.E.I. rangers on the Peninsula.

Even "traditional" camping has changed more than by just the expansion of the artist's palette to include fluorescent colors. The hue and cry of modern explorers is "brighter and lighter." A quick trip to any outdoor recreation store will provide you with the insight to define that catch phrase.

The "brighter" part refers to the most garish color schemes imaginable, generally based on a purple and chartreuse theme. The professed intent of the colors is to make camping a more cheerful experience, but the resultant effect just scares the bejabbers out of any wild creature with even a modicum of vision.

The "lighter" part refers to the technological advancements in design, construction and materials. Those advancements combine to reduce the weight of your wallet. The "lighter" quality of the new gear puts a cramp on rough and tumble camping experiences. It's not that the equipment can't take it, mind you, it's just that the thought of trashing something that cost as much as a three bedroom, two bath home, with Jacuzzi and sauna, gives most folks pause for thought. More often than not, while folks with kids are pausing to think, someone sells them a version of that home-- one with wheels.

As nice as tradition is, many people find that the natural course of things takes them away from traditional camping. Marriage and having children evolves the camping experience into a completely different situation. This evolution is no different than the trend experienced by the early settlers.

The first explorers carried only what they needed on their trips with, perhaps, the aid of a horse. With just bedrolls and packs, everything they needed could be toted quite handily. These people were satisfied without taking all the trappings of civilization with them. Eventually however, the westward movement became a family thing, and the law of inverse packing proportions was discovered. Simply stated, the law of inverse packing proportions is the smaller and younger the camper, the bigger the pile of camping necessities. With the discovery of this law came the Conestoga wagon.

As traditionalists discover the law of inverse packing proportions, just as our forefathers did, they resort to the same solution. They fall back to the Conestoga of the Twentieth Century, the motor home.

Every weekend on the Peninsula offers the opportunity to sit alongside the road and be treated to a reenactment of the great wagon trains of old. Just as the pioneers would wind their lines of Conestogas through the passes, seeking the wide open expanses of the wilderness, so do the long stretches of Winnebago, upon Pace Arrow, upon Tioga, upon Cruise Aire.

Oh, how I love historical reenactments! I know, deep in my heart, that our great-great-grandfathers rode their horses behind a long string of Conestogas passing through their towns, cursing the snail's pace all the while.

"Great! Another wagon train. I just *hate* when they get stacked up like this. They think they own the damn trail. Hey! C'mon buddy, *move it!* Whatcha' got under the yoke, a Shetland pony?"

The really big difference between the occupants of the old wagon trains and the modern ones is that the pioneers had plenty of room to head into. They had the entire wilderness. If it happened that someone beat the driver of the Conestoga to a parking place, there was always another one, just up the trail. Today's Conestogas don't have that option.

If, in the frontier days, a pioneer family found all the prime parking places taken, and they couldn't continue (either physically or mentally) they simply "squatted" a piece of land off someone else. Today's version is the "shopping mall" camper. Those are the folks that simply give up after several attempts at finding a place in the local campgrounds and settle in at the nearest shopping mall parking lot. There are advantages to "squatting" a shopping mall: handy groceries, easy access to any spare part needed, and fewer people than at the popular fishing holes.

Camping has been and will continue to be one of America's favorite pastimes. I'm glad we can go back in history to enjoy ourselves every Friday when it's time to load up the kids, and check the air in the wagon wheels.

You Can Lead Your Wife to Water
(But You Shouldn't Make Her Fish)

Most of us who enjoy the outdoors-- and by outdoors I mean more in particular fishing-- sometimes unwisely try to generate the same enthusiasm in other individuals. On several occasions, my personal attempts to initiate someone to the good life has ended just short of disaster. My last such attempt should serve as a warning to others in the fishing fraternity.

My wife, Georgia, has been forgiving and understanding about my all-consuming passion for fishing since we first met. It defies science to explain how two people can live in such an intimate relationship, raise two children, and in a pinch, even share a toothbrush, while only one remains infected with fishing fever. In reflecting upon that one day, I decided to correct the situation.

Previously, Georgia would accompany me on fishing trips only under protest, and generally whiled away the time with a book on the shore. Even the most spectacular of my catches elicited no more than a casual glance and an impartial, "That's nice." Things were about to change.

The first step was to try and instill a little personal pride in the ownership of a fine fishing rig. It is indeed fortunate that my wife's parents planned her birthday in the spring, as it offered the perfect opportunity to instill her with pride. After a great deal of thought, and numerous trips to the local tackle shops, a beautiful ball bearing reel was matched with an exceptionally sensitive graphite rod. As I left the shop, I couldn't help but hope Georgia would like for us to have a matching set, just to increase the togetherness.

Any sensible individual can imagine my surprise when the present was received with a cool response. I was accused of repeating a faux pas of earlier years when I purchased a nice twelve gauge shotgun for our son's first birthday (which is, coincident-ally, one week before duck season). Then the discussion turned to the time that I chartered a fly-in trip for our daughter on her fourth birthday (in my haste to make reservations, I only booked one seat).

When I explained that I had just bought a new roll of duct tape to repair my own rod and reel, her suspicions were somewhat allayed. It took a bit more to stifle the raucous laughter of the children.

The second step was to get Georgia to use the equipment that she was now so proud of. It was several days before she would even talk about trying out her new rig. We discussed the importance of style, and I demonstrated the correct technique for precision placement. The effect of the lecture was lost when I placed the tip of the rod precisely through the center of her grandmother's silk lamp shade.

Finally, after much prodding on my part, Georgia admitted that she just didn't want to get her shiny new rig dirty, so I promised that we would practice in the front yard where the grass is very clean. There were a few bird's nests, and a couple of casts went awry, ending up in the trees. But Georgia is a quick student, and when I gave her the pole, she did just fine.

The aesthetics of lure selection seemed to be the most difficult for her to grasp. The difference between a spoon and a spinner was not important, and the two were interchangeable in her opinion. With that philosophy in mind, the choice of color or pattern was even less important. We debated the use of salmon eggs, but ultimately ruled their use out as they "make your hands stink." I was finally forced to agree that the selection could be made strictly on the basis if what was easiest to cast, but emphasized that a half-ounce jig was not applicable to every situation.

At that point, the futility of explaining lure selection based on structure, or even an explanation of structure itself, became painfully apparent. My frustration would have made me give up at this point, but Georgia said, "Let's forget the academics, and go kill some fish."

The glint in her eyes was heartening, but I made a mental note that a lecture on catch and release was needed.

The trout were moving in the shallows of the lakes around our house, and nearby Douglas Lake was the logical place to take her. It offered not only easy access, but clear visibility. I reasoned that if she could see the fish strike, the excitement of her first catch would be enhanced.

There were several encouraging swirls on the water as we approached the edge of the lake. I explained that the trout were spawning, and that it was imperative to release the fish correctly so no injury would occur. She smiled and explained that was why I was along. I didn't worry as she tied on her jig, but was amazed later at how far out and deep the really big trout were.

During one of my warm up periods, (May waters are still very cold to the hands) she asked me when the king salmon would start running. I allowed that she had learned quickly about the techniques for trout, but that fishing for a king was an entirely different situation. In addition to that, I reminded her that there was only one king rig in the household. I was in turn reminded that it took one person to run the boat, which left one person to fish. I was also reminded of the times that my one rig had been sufficient for her brother and I when he was up visiting, and the numerous other times one rig had been enough when I had been obligated to take friends out. I was beginning to regret the emphasis I had placed on watching other fishermen to learn their tricks.

The end of June found our family unit in total disarray. The usual routine of coming home from work and spending a quiet evening meal with the kids had been replaced with a salami sandwich shoved in my face as we made tracks for the river. We couldn't have eaten at the table anyway, all of Georgia's snelling and leader tying gear had long since replaced the condiments and place mats.

By mid-July, Georgia was in a full lather, and still had not taken a king. Matters were worsened by the fact that I had yet to have a chance to get a line in the water. This led to the inevitable confrontation that all married couples have now and then to 'clear the air' and keep the lines of communication open. However, most married folks don't run their boat up on a rock in the process. The *Doghouse* was a complete loss. The elusive king would have to be stalked from the bank.

Our socks had barely dried when we went to the local tackle shop to replace the lost gear. This time two rigs were purchased.

The second run of kings was peaking when we found ourselves at the mouth of a small creek that empties into the Kenai. We set up our Spin 'N Glos with eggs in an eddy behind a large rock. I had just settled in to wait for the tap that sends you to your feet, when Georgia jumped up and set her hook. The line went slack. Her moan had barely died away when the fish hit again. It's a good thing that she connected the second time, or the fall would have resulted in a serious injury.

The fish took extreme exception to the rough handling, and headed downstream with all the strength it could muster. The reel sounded like and amplified dentist's drill, and I could barely make out Georgia's, "Do something!"

It's odd that a man will look back on his life to discover that some of what seemed to be the most logical things to do, were actually the most stupid. I had just barely tweeked the reel's drag when the loudest pop I have ever heard from fishing line stopped all the commotion.

Georgia turned slowly to face me fully, "I just set that drag before we started."

A young couple just upstream from us had watched all this. The man went back to fishing, and his wife went back to reading her book. Georgia walked over to them and handed her rig to the young lady.

"Here honey," Georgia said with a twisted smile, "this will give you two something to talk about at length."

The Secret of Stable Canoes

By and far, the most commonly owned water craft in Alaska is the canoe. It is almost a requirement to own a canoe in order to have the right to call yourself an outdoors enthusiast. Even people that have fancy, fully rigged boats with console controls, hydraulic lifts on the motors, and snap on canopies, have an old canoe stashed away somewhere. There is a simple explanation for this: people get smarter over the years.

Canoes have been in use by Native Americans for eons. The first canoes were probably fashioned by hollowing out large logs. This did two things: it made it easier to drag the log out of the water when not in use, and made the log more challenging to ride. Eventually, somebody figured out how to save a lot of work and make the canoe much lighter while still maintaining the basic instability: one simply peeled the skin from a tree instead of scraping the innards out.

The new, easy mileage models were constructed of wood frames covered with birch bark. The birch pieces were sewn together with roots, and caulked with resin. I would imagine that only childless, slim, non-smokers could get their canoes insured back then.

Great improvements in construction materials have been made, and now instead of just the basic white birch with black resin stripes model, just about any color can be had from fluorescent yellow to camouflage. The new materials also make it possible to carelessly step into a canoe instead of through the canoe.

Even with all the new materials, the traditional long and low shape of the canoe hasn't really changed much. It's still true that the best thing about a canoe is that it's so low to the water that when the inevitable fall comes, it won't hurt you. A sleek double-ender exudes a look of eagerness for movement. It just hasn't made its mind up as to which way to go, with both ends being pointed.

The streamlined design allows for maneuverability. Canoes can, and do, change course readily. Frequently without the benefit of any conscious effort on the part of the paddlers. Were it not for the canoe's ability to make quick turns, many of the river boulders I have encountered would have been missed entirely.

The thought of having a canoe is one of those special ideas that is great until one tries to put it into practice. The biggest selling feature of the canoe is its portability. Everyone that is selling a used canoe will expound at length on the marvelous ease of its portability. But even in transportation stability is a problem.

"Yeah, and the best thing about this baby is how easy it is to transport. You just toss it up on top of the car and go. No trailer, none of those hassles."

"Sounds great. Say, how'd that side get all banged up?"

"Oh, just a little problem with one of the tie downs. Did I tell you that I could load this thing all by myself? It doesn't weigh but about sixty-five pounds. Just grab it..."

"Is that the vehicle you used to haul it around with?"

"Yeah. It's so simple to just grab the..."

"Pretty nasty looking scrape on the side of the roof. Do that with the canoe?"

"Just feel how lightweight this baby is."

Generally, the just throw it on top and go theory of transporting canoes is a good deal smoother than the practical application. Most canoes are the perfect length to be just a little too long, or a little too short to be tied down securely. There's always enough play in the ropes, no matter how tightly one cinches them down initially, that enough slop will develop in less than a quarter mile of travel to allow the canoe to slide around like an ice cube on a hot griddle. Bumpy roads can easily convert that "easy to transport" cargo into a side mounted baggage pod.

162

The basic shape of a canoe may allow it to gracefully slide through the water, but wind speeds over thirty miles per hour make it act like a huge top-mounted rudder on a vehicle. This effect at speeds above fifty miles per hour, coupled with a minimal cross wind, creates a serpentine motion that would be the envy of any slalom skier. With a good, stiff head wind, it's possible to weave between *all* the yellow stripes.

Once the navigable waters are reached, the new owner's *mental* stability can be jeopardized. Paddling a canoe can be an exercise in frustration for the novice.

"Okay, you steer the canoe from the stern."

"Which end is the stern?"

"The end with the seat closest to the tip of the canoe. Of course, that is, unless you want to paddle by yourself. Then the bow is the stern."

"Okay. The stern is the back unless I'm by myself, then the front is the stern."

"Right. Now let's get in, and give it a try. You steer."

"Okay, let's see. The seat closest to... Oh, after you. I'll shove off."

The actual strokes are simple to learn, and soon enough, anyone can be creeping along, wobbling and balancing on a meandering course.

Lack of speed is the canoe's biggest drawback, and has resulted in the only design modification in the past millennium or two of use. One end was lopped off square. This was not done strictly for aesthetic appeal, although it does actually make them look like they know where they're going and help people decide which end to sit in.

No, the "square stern" canoe was developed with a much more ominous idea in mind. It made it possible to equip a craft designed for hand propulsion with a motor. This marvelous modification did nothing for the canoe's stability, but it did make it possible to tip over while traveling at a dangerously high rate of speed.

Since many of us like to frequent places that aren't as popular as the Kenai River, which pretty much demands the use of a boat, we are stuck with canoes. For years, a means to stabilize our crafts has eluded us, but no more. There is a secret way to do it.

It seems that the only way to stabilize a canoe is with ballast, lots of ballast. The first layer should be gravel, followed by fill, and topped with a good quality peat. Since I learned this secret, my canoe hasn't tipped over on me for two years. I don't have any transportation problems, and I'm generally all by myself in the backyard as I sit and admire the flowers that are enhanced by the sleek lines of the craft that holds them. Steadily.

Golfing Around

Recently, I have been asked by no less than three people if I play golf. There seems to be an heightened interest in golf in Alaska in the past couple of years. I attribute it to the aging of the residents. The average age in Alaska is increasing, and as we all get older, the physical demands of the rugged outdoor activities that used to occupy our spare time seem to get more difficult to meet. (As an example, Knucks Mahoneigh was whining just the other day about how badly his knees ached when he climbed the steps into his motor-home.)

I'm not one of those people. I'm getting older, but I don't mind doing outdoor things at a slower pace. To me, it's hard to fathom why someone would want to spend the short summer in Alaska playing golf.

Let's give this some thought. How many times, when planning a trip to Alaska, does the question, "So, which golf course shall we play first," come up? I would suspect very few, if ever. People don't think of Alaska in terms of golf.

Picture the returning Alaskan tourists, Muffy and Biff. They are arriving back home after a wonderful vacation in the Greatland, decked out in their brand new tourist tee shirts, low cut boat mocassins, and sporting that beautiful faded tan look people from the Lower Forty-eight pick up while vacationing here. Their friends, Dexter and Bubbles, have come to the airport to give them a ride home.

"You guys look positively washed out. How was the trip?"

"Oh, just fantastic! The scenery was unbelievable, but the courses were just so-so."

"What'd you shoot?"

"Well, believe it or not, one day I shot three eagles."

At this point, five burly men jump out of the woodwork and shout in unison, "*Freeze, maggot!* U.S. Fish and Wildlife. You're under arrest for the federal crime of killing eagles."

Muffy and Biff are taken aback, to say the least. "Killing eagles? No, no, I shot three eagles."

The biggest guy in the neatly pressed uniform takes charge. "Read him his rights, Burt. We don't want to blow this case with an inadmissible confession."

As two other agents assist Biff into a leaning position against the nearest wall and start patting him down, he tries to explain the misunderstanding. "Wait! Wait! What I meant was..."

"There you go. He's already trying to weasel out of it."

"You don't understand. *I was playing golf!*"

The big guy just gives Biff that patented lawman's glare. "Right. You went to Alaska, and played golf. I've heard it all. Cuff him. You can tell it to the judge. Probably go for an insanity plea. Thought he was playing golf in Alaska. That's good... that's really rich."

See what I mean? Golf just doesn't fit the Alaskan image. Golf is something people do down south because the fish don't bite during the heat of the day.

Golf doesn't fit in with the frontier image either. Although the rustic Alaskan male persona (hyped by certain magazines intended primarily for distribution to single women in the Lower Forty-eight) is a bit overplayed, at least it fits into the scenery. Golf is too genteel.

Most Alaskans aren't hung up on the need to participate in macho sports simply to project an image. But even so, golf is a game one has to wonder about. There is something about a sport that forces men to wear tassels on their shoes that is discomforting. Listening to the description of courses such as "rugged" or "tough" or even "strenuous" when uttered by men that haven't even broken a sweat also gives one pause for thought. And the old line about getting exercise with this particular sport is shot down the tubes

166

when the first thing one sees upon arrival at a course is the row of carts used to ride across those neatly trimmed grassy stretches between tee and green.

"Yeah, I'll take one of those carts over there. Since I play this game for the exercise, you better give me one without power steering."

It is equally difficult to swallow the reasoning behind the "I play golf to relax," statement. I know a few golfers, and the vocabulary they use to describe their last game is normally not indicative of one who is relaxed. Golf is perhaps one of the most difficult games in which to develop a true level of skill while maintaining your sanity.

As if the inherent negative aspects of the sport were not enough to convince folks that golf isn't such a good idea up here, there are additional obstacles to be surmounted when playing in the Greatland.

The first is the weather. Down south when it starts to rain, golfers head for cover. If Alaskan golfers gave up everytime it started to rain, they might complete a nine hole round once every decade. Fortunately the type of rain we get up here isn't normally like the drenching downpours that are found down south, nor do the golfers up here become walking lightning rods. Still, it's difficult to imagine looking out the window on a rainy day and thinking that the perfect way to spend the day would be to wander around in the mist and drizzle, whacking a little white ball in and out of dense vegetation. (If you have that thought frequently, I urge you to seek professional help.)

The rain provides Alaskans with another handicap: the mosquito. It's bad enough that there will be lots of mosquitoes on the fairways, but drive a ball into a brushy rough, and the situation provides a new definition to the term "blood sport." Most folks gladly take the penalty and wait until after the first frost to look for lost balls.

Another handicap Alaskan golfers have is moose. Golf courses are almost as good as vegetable gardens for attracting moose. The best rule of thumb is to always let the moose play through, no matter how long it takes.

All of this leads us to the answer of the question, do I play golf? Not any more.

In the bliss and ignorance of my youth there were times that I didn't have enough stress and frustration in my daily routine, so I played golf to prepare myself for parenthood. Having grown a little older, the need for self-inflicted stress disappeared, and was replaced with a genuine need to do something to lower my blood pressure.

As a suitable, and infinitely more relaxing substitute, I have taken to trimming my toenails with a chainsaw.

Gold Fever

There really isn't anyone to blame but Johnny Horton. He is responsible for a great deal of the loneliness in my life. If it weren't for having heard his song "North to Alaska" in my impressionable youth, the thought of seeking gold probably never would have entered my mind. That song was the one about how Big Sam McCord, George Pratt and Brother Billy all set out to find their fortune during the gold rush. That was when men were really men, and a guy could truly be an independent provider. There weren't any quiche eaters in the Yukon, buster. What a life! With little sweat, a person could be set forever in nothing flat.

According to the song, it would appear there is little more involved in the accumulation of gold than bending over and picking up the overly abundant nuggets that adorn the stream and river beds of Alaska. There were other subjects in the song, too. Old George suffered from a propensity to whine at length about his girl and such, but if you lopped out the mushy stuff, and got right down to it, the song was about all the gold you could get in Alaska. Unfortunately, it was only the bit about gathering up bucketfuls of gold that I heard. What should have stood out was poor old George's lamentations about his girl.

Talk to someone who is an active recreational miner, and they will enthusiastically explain that gold is found almost anywhere in Alaska. With a fervor that leaves them all but breathless, they will convince any and all who will listen that a shovel, a gold pan, and a "little practice" is all that's needed to begin collecting a fortune.

Panning is simply a method to separate gold, in the form of flakes or nuggets, from the dirt it is found in. It works on the theory that gold is heavier than the surrounding dirt, and will therefore settle to the bottom of the pan. Mother Nature proves this theory out by getting the gold to settle into pockets. These pockets are usually located: a) at least twenty feet below the surface of the earth, or b) just below a few inches of easy to remove gravel that is located in the middle of a swift, freezing cold torrent of water. This helps in pinpointing exactly where one would want to pan. It's simply a matter of looking for the most inaccessible place. After that, one just starts moving dirt.

Knowing when it is time to stop digging, and start panning is easy. Start separating your fortune when: a) the danger of burial from a cave-in exists, or b) when water is lapping at the top of your chest waders.

The act of panning is simplicity itself. Put a shovelful of dirt in the pan, add water and gently swirl the mess around. Now thump the edge of the pan. The first motion is to get the gold to settle out. The second motion is to regain some feeling back in the fingers. Tipping the pan allows the lighter dirt to wash out. After that, it's time to scoop the load back up or get a new shovelful.

That same process is repeated over and over. Eventually, the original shovelful will be reduced to just a small amount of material. This material, called black sand, is where the gold will be found. Swirling the black sand around the bottom of the pan with just a little water gets the heavier gold particles to separate by trailing just behind.

See it? Look closer. Get your face right down into the pan. Use one eye, maybe that will help. Try squinting. Nothing? Try another shovelful. It's there, you just haven't found it yet.

All this sure makes a person appreciate what the old timers went through. It also makes clear why old George was whining and carrying on in the song. Who would want to do this all by themselves? It's true, when having this much fun, misery loves company.

In addition to the purely academic assessment of pioneer life and having such a great time, there exists another good reason for taking to the local gold fields. Gold panning is the married Alaskan's equivalent of the cheap date.

Weekend gold panning doesn't require much capital to initiate, and there is a possibility, albeit remote, of a small return on the investment. Why, I even know a guy who found enough gold flake in three summers to pay for the new glasses he needed from the eye strain of looking in his pan.

The biggest problem encountered by the would-be gold seeker today is the same problem the early prospectors had: getting a modicum of moral support for the venture.

From personal experience, I do not recommend sweeping your significant other into your arms, and romantically murmuring the line, "C'mon Baby, let's have us a cheap date and go panning this weekend."

In fact, I would suspect it was that very sort of thing that led George Pratt to his lonely life of hanging out with just Big Sam and company.

No, a modern, sensitive, Nineties kind of guy must approach the situation with a different tack. "Hon, let's get away together. How does a quiet weekend of camping sound? We could really bond." (The word "bond" is important here. "Bonding" is really in now.)

Another good way to get some cooperative company is to visit one of the local stores selling natural gold nugget jewelry. While admiring the beauty and luster of the natural gold nuggets, casually mention that kind of gold is available for just a little effort. Maybe you could mumble just a couple of the first few lines from "North to Alaska." I particularly like the part about winding rivers and finding big nuggets. (It's important, however, not to get mired down in old George's monologue. In fact, if your intended partner starts joining in, switch songs immediately.)

With either of those approaches, there is no way that a negative response will be heard. Faster than the shovel and pans can be thrown into the prospector's rig, your intended companion will be heading down the trail to riches seeking the mother lode... at least the first time. If anybody knows about something that might work for a second trip, I'd like to hear about it.

Vehicular Recognition as a Social Function

Everything is spread out around here. In order to buy groceries, see a movie, go bowling or do something cultural like take in the local hockey team, it's not uncommon to drive thirty miles. That amounts to a lot of time in the family vehicle. Taking the amount of time spent on the roads, and the fact that we don't have that many roads to pick and choose from, traveling around locally becomes, in itself, a social thing. You may not have the time to go over to a friend's house, but you can always socialize with them on the road.

This aspect of transportation can cause stress. If one doesn't live up to his or her social obligations there could be repercussions. Neighbors might think you're unfriendly, and friends might think that you're ticked-off about something. Sometimes, between the house and the post office, I feel like I'm sitting in for the beauty queen of a large parade: right hand up, slowly waving back and forth, head tilted jauntily to one side, a broad grin plastered on my face. "Hi there! How are you? Fine, thanks. Oops! Can't wave, gotta shift. Okay, where were we? Better yet, where'd you go?"

Lots of things can go wrong with this socializing process. One of them is slow reflexes. Frequently, my slow reflexes result in a hearty wave to strangers that are driving behind the people I know.

The social responsibility to appear friendly and show recognition on time is strong. The kids have picked up on this, much to their amusement. They have discovered that by saying,

"Wave, Dad," any time another vehicle is close, my right hand will shoot up. A sort of Pavlov's Driver reflex.

A delayed or miscued wave such as that can cause much confusion in the resulting chain reaction. If it happens to be summer, and there is much traffic, all sorts of people make new friends. Some are from out of state. No wonder visitors comment on how friendly Alaskans are.

At one time, in a mood of total determination, I made mental flash cards of all our friends and their respective vehicles. Running down the list in my mind, I would leave the house confident that no faux pas in vehicular socialization would be committed.

That was three years ago. I now wave merrily to the new owners of several of those vehicles.

Personal experience has shown that I'm not the only one who has problems of this nature. A couple of years back, we bought an old pickup for hauling trash and whatnot. The previous owner's son must have been a genuine stud muffin. Even in the prime of my youth, that many young ladies never noticed me. It was nice, until the young ladies got close enough to realize it was just me. Those looks of abject disappointment were crushing. I soon grew tired of hauling garbage only at night to protect my ego, and that truck was quickly sold. One potential buyer thought I was nuts when I refused to sell it to him just because he was newly married, but it was for his own good.

Used cars and trucks aren't the only vehicles that present a problem. Someone should pass an ordinance limiting the number of new vehicles sold that are identical. There are a limited number of new car dealers, selling a limited number of models, in a limited number of colors. This causes an unlimited amount of embarrassment.

A case in point is when a couple I know, Ross and Annie, bought a new blue and silver mini-van. It was so pretty, that a few months later someone else got one just like it. That should not present a problem-- just glance at the driver. Except that Annie is blonde, so is the owner of the other mini-van. Waiting to get a look at the face results in the delayed reflex syndrome.

Nuts to it. Let me take this opportunity to set the record straight. To the owner of the blue and silver mini-van on the North

174

Road, from the wildly waving idiot in the white Vista: it's nothing personal, I'm just trying to be social.

There was a brief ray of hope for easy identification when those fluorescent colored windshield wipers came out. It was my plan to give them out as gifts of one sort or another. It was a good idea, just wave to those cars that glowed. Hard to miss, and the mistakes would be minimal. Unfortunately, the enthusiasm they were received with by friends was limited, to say the least.

"Oh, why thank you. A pair of, uh... unusual wipers. Too bad they won't fit. Don't worry, I'll take them back myself."

Really, I guess when taken in with the big scheme of things, salutations on the roadway aren't much to worry about. Most everyone here is friendly enough to forgive a forgotten wave, and appreciate a friendly mistaken wave.

I grew up in big cities. I have driven quite a bit in big cities. Most of the drivers in big cities that have waved at me, only bothered to use one finger.

So, the next time you spend time cruising the roads in Alaska, and see some red-faced fool wave at you, just do the social thing and wave back.

Fear of Canning

By August, it's time for my annual late summer anxiety attack. I realize that it is an irrational fear, and I know full well that many will snort in disgust at my cowardice. I am also sure that there is some fancy medical phrase for my phobia that would make it sound horrible enough to generate some sort of sympathy, but there is no need to sugarcoat the situation. To me, the fear is real, and it is adequate to call it just what it is. I have a fear of canning. I'm sure that I'm not alone with this situation, I'm just more honest than most.

Alaska is no place to have qualms about preserving food by canning. Since many Alaskans use what nature provides for a substantial portion of their food supply, preservation for extended storage is a necessity. Canning salmon is the Alaskan equivalent of coupon clipping before grocery shopping. While folks in the Lower Forty-eight swap tales of fantastic buys-- such as two-for-one and buy one, get six gross for free-- Alaskans brag on the quantity of salmon they have canned. Not canning salmon has relegated me to the position of social leper during the months of August and September.

First off, let's explore a question about the term "canning" that has plagued me for quite some time. If one takes some sort of organic material, stuffs it into a metal can, steam blasts it into the consistency of oatmeal, and then seals the can, I can see why it is called canning. What bothers me is that many people do all the stuffing and steam blasting with glass jars and then insist on calling it canning.

I would suppose that calling fish put up in glass jars, "jarred" fish could cause a little confusion on the beach.

"Say Bud, you gonna jar that fish?"

"I already did. Jarred him smack b'twixt the eyes with a rock as soon as I got him to shore. He floppin' around again?"

I digress. See how difficult it is to face a fear the magnitude of "the fear of canning?"

Having a fear of canning isn't as convenient as having something as widely accepted as claustrophobia. If you should happen to mention in passing that you are claustrophobic, people will go out of their way to accomodate you. Try it out. Next time you're in an elevator, fidget a little by bouncing from foot to foot and wringing your hands. Then mention in an off-handed way, "Gee, I hope this thing doesn't get stuck between floors. I've got claustrophobia." Everyone will instantly remember that they had pressing business on the very next floor.

The treatment is much different if the fear of canning is involved. Out dipnetting, some unfeeling clod will bring up canning the catch. "Oh man! The old canner is gonna get a work-out now, isn't it?"

"Uh... well, no. I just fillet and freeze 'em."

"You can't be serious. You don't can your fish? They won't be any good after a couple of months. Say, you aren't one of those canning sissies, are you?"

Canning is dangerous business. Canning requires the use of an item that has all the potential destructive power of a small nuclear warhead. Canning involves pressure cookers. People, folks we normally consider sane, rational and careful persons keep these things in their homes. They even let their children get near them for God's sake! What can these people be thinking?

As I said, I know there are others like myself out there. It just stands to reason, because there were too many of us mentally scarred in our youth with the advent of the pressure cooker, the microwave of the fifties.

What a boon to the housewife. What a labor saving device. Why, with one handy little cooking utensil, a five pound potroast, six big potatoes and a quart of fresh peas could be cooked in less than half an hour. I even remember the demonstrations. There, right out in the open, where hundreds could have been maimed, some petite lady in a gingham dress would prepare a complete meal for a family of thirty-seven. The manufacturers were betting that the crowd wouldn't take notice of the half dozen or so burly gentlemen milling around in their flak jackets in case the situation got out of control. Most people didn't. My mother was one of them.

My mother loved her shiny, new *Blammo!* pressure cooker. Every meal was a delectable testimonial to the power of steam generation. At last she had found a way to save time so that it was possible to do all the things moms were saddled with back before liberation. A balanced, nourishing meal was possible every day in nothing flat. And if the urge struck her, she could hold an entire city block hostage by putting the thing on high boil.

There were only two real failures that I remember. The first was an honest mistake, but it led to the second, which was the grand finale for pressure cooking in the our household, and the basis for my fear of you know what.

Actually, Dad had to share some of the blame. Every Thursday was fried cabbage and bacon night. We would all hold our noses while Mom would fry up the disgusting concoction so it would be waiting when Dad got home.

One Thursday, Mom got a little sidetracked over a minor incident involving a couple of turtles and the clothes dryer. Before she knew it, Dad was due home.

To make a bad situation short, let's just summarize by saying that pressure frying does not work.

Dad was a little disappointed, but a substitute dinner could be steamed up in just a few minutes, just as soon as Mom sandblasted the bacon and cabbage out of the old Blammo miracle cooker. Unfortunately, the cabbage and bacon splatterings that had sealed the "safety relief device" (which consisted of an aluminum plug set onto a vent in the lid) went unnoticed in the quick turnaround necessary to get the pressure cooker back on line.

Mom threw the usual ingredients for a standard miracle meal into the Blammo while Dad and I sat in the living room and discussed what I had learned about turtles that very day. She had no sooner left the blast zone to join us, commenting about how it would be ready quicker than usual because she really cranked up the heat, when a horrific blast sent us all reeling. (To this very day, I have nightmares about headlines in the paper grimly proclaiming, *Family Maimed in Pressure Cooker Accident*.) Dinner was literally on the house, mostly the ceiling, around the big hole.

We patched the hole and cleaned up as best we could, but for years every now and then a new remnant of a pea would catch your eye. Painting didn't help. The pea color would work its way through.

So you see, my fear is really based on an experience that left a scarring impression. The thought of a salmon pink kitchen gives me cold sweats.

Weight Loss

Alaska is a land of extremes. We experience extreme swings in daylight, extreme swings in temperature, and extreme swings in preoccupations. Fall is the time to kick off the annual weight loss/gain preoccupation.

This seems a little odd to the uninitiated observer. After a summer of outdoor activity, Alaskans should have no thoughts about weight loss. Summer is a prime example of an Alaskan extreme. From May through Labor Day, Alaskans spend as much time as possible on the go and outside. One would think all that exercise while being in the great outdoors would have kept pace with even the heartiest of caloric intakes.

Unfortunately, just being in the outdoors puts weight on most people. Really. What's the first thing people say when they go out camping? "There's something about being out in this fresh air that sparks my appetite."

Looking at the average shopping cart on a Thursday before a camping trip explains it all. There will be several two- pounder bags of chips, a couple bags of candy bars, assorted cookies, a case or two of soda, at least one bag of marshmallows, a ten pound bag of potatoes, tubs of butter, two to six packages of hotdogs, pancake mix, syrup and on and on. That's just for a two day weekend.

The truly scary part about this is that there are rarely any leftovers from a camping trip. Alaskans favor a "take no prisoners" attitude toward their camping groceries.

It's not a simple matter of gluttony that encourages this mass consumption. Envision the average summer camping trip. The family arrives at the campsite, sets things up, gets the fire pit all squared away, and then the rain starts. As the family huddles under the tarp, or in a tent or camper, something has to be done to help pass the time.

"Hey! Let's go for a hike!"

"What're you, nuts? If you step out from under the tarp, the rain'll pound you flat. Pass the chips."

"Guess you're right... by the way, the chips are gone. Here, have another Twinkie."

Fishing packs on the extra poundage too. With all the activity of climbing in the boat, and riding up and down the river, a person can work up a real appetite. The problem is, space is limited, so the meal has to be compact. Most fish slayers that I know maintain a common philosophy on nutrition and fishing.

"I never take a meal with me when I fish. Don't have time or room. I usually just take a dozen or so candy bars. Gotta keep the ol' energy level up, ya know."

So, why all the concern about summer belly blossom now? The oncoming winter and resultant period of sloth provides the answer. It is a simple fact that by the time spring finally rolls around, so do a lot of Alaskans. Anyone who has been here long enough to have grown tired of dashing through the snow also knows that the odds on bet is that one of the resolutions made by January is to trim off some of the extra weight. The general idea is to start now and get ahead of the game.

As is the case with most other situations that involve some sort of self improvement, some well-meaning soul (that generally did not suffer any damage from the summer flab fairy) decides that everybody's personal weight predicament deserves public involvement. This most often occurs at the workplace, and takes the guise of some sort of contest.

These contests have rules such as:

"If the minimum loss is not met each week by weigh in, the contestant will pay the contest kitty one percent of their take-home pay. If more than the required weight is lost, it may be banked against the following week's loss but may not be carried over to subsequent weeks. If the contestant fails to lose the prescribed weight for two consecutive weeks, one week's vacation will be forfeit. Should the contestant actually *gain* weight, they will be discharged following a public flogging."

Of course, just to ensure total fairness, the contest weigh-ins are monitored by someone who has peanut M&M's on their breath and was a former foldout for *Anorexic Babes Magazine*.

During this public weight loss contest the focus of the preoccupations shift. Instead of everyone quietly walking around concerned with just their own weight loss program, the focus of the conversations shift to how others' weight loss is going.

Suddenly, gone are the days of a friendly "Hello." Now it's, "Whoa, have you been to weigh-in yet? Lookin' a little close there, maybe you oughta call in sick."

All of this preoccupation and pressure to lose has produced an entire industry based on separating individuals from their waistbands and money. Fad diets abound. You can starve on a nutritionally balanced plan of one sort or another for almost any amount you care to spend. One is pretty much like the other. They all create a situation that makes food-- any food-- desirable. I actually found myself drooling when I was reading *From Here to Eternity* while on a diet. I could almost taste that bread and water those lucky stiffs in solitary got to eat.

Actually, all that's needed to provide steady weight loss and a chance to win the contest (thereby saving your job and security in old age) is good self-discipline from the start, and the Poynor Plumbum Plan. This plan is one hundred percent guaranteed to help take off exactly what weight is needed, easily and without hunger pains.

It's a simple, can't miss program. Just follow these easy steps. Prior to the initial weigh in, make a belt out of halibut fishing sinkers to slip on under your shirt. During the course of the following weeks, eat as you normally would, and take off only the weight you need.

Time Passes

Time is the friend of no person. In fact, time is the universal enemy of all people. How should an enemy be treated? Well, according to G. Khan of Lake Baikal, Mongolia, an enemy should not be defeated, he should be crushed and utterly destroyed.

That pretty well sums up what time does to us, and as if crushing and destroying us weren't enough, twice a year, time is also given the opportunity to humiliate us.

The biannual "Humiliation by Time" is celebrated in April, and again in October. The celebration centers around forcing the general public to alter their timepieces and their biological clocks by an hour. I can't understand why, as Alaskans, we tolerate this abuse.

Who is responsible for this malicious practice? Most sources claim that Benjamin Franklin was the first to suggest it in 1784. His rationale reportedly being that it would save candles. This idea was bought wholesale by our government in 1960 (a time at which candle sales were experiencing an historic peak, no doubt).

What a deal. It took our government one hundred seventy-six years to decide to take the advice of some guy who was known to fly kites in lightning storms (and let it be noted that he actually came up with the idea for saving candles *after* the lightning hit his kite). Personally, I think the invention of the light bulb probably saved a lot more candles. But what do I know?

As if forcing us to change our lives around twice a year wasn't enough, the rules of the celebration dictate that the clocks be changed at two in the morning. Now, that makes sense. During the spring change, we're supposed to get up at two so we can lose an hour's sleep. In addition, there's the sleep that's lost in worrying about not getting back to sleep after waking up in the middle of the night to short yourself on sleep. In the fall, we're supposed to interrupt our rest to pick up an extra hour that will be lost trying to go back to sleep. Who the hell wrote these rules, anyway?

One of the amazing things about Daylight Saving is the amount of confusion generated with each change. How unpopular the changes are can be judged by the fact that many people never bother to learn which direction the clocks are supposed to be turned on the given day.

"Uh-oh, it's time to switch the clocks again... do we lose an hour or pick one up?"

"Lemme see... spring ahead, fall down. No... spring up, fall through. That's not it. Spring away..."

"How about we just call time and temperature when we get up, and see if we're late for church?"

Of course, the sensible thing to do is to set the clocks before retiring. Not only is this sensible, it also offers some opportunity for fun in the spring. After moving the clocks ahead, someone will undoubtedly call. This provides a prime opportunity to be surly about how late they waited to call.

One wouldn't think that an hour's difference in a daily routine would be all that much, but it seems to have adverse impacts. The key to overcoming the adversity is mental attitude. One must take a positive approach to the situation. You are getting up at the same time, only later, and the sun isn't setting earlier, it's setting faster.

All this brings us to the most baffling thing about Daylight Saving. Why do Alaskans even bother with this nonsense? What point is there for us to go along with the notion that we're "saving daylight?"

When the switch to save daylight is made in April, Alaskans are already working with an overabundance. What is accomplished by moving sunrise from five-thirty to six-thirty and sunset from eight-thirty to nine-thirty? We get more evening hours of daylight to sit out on the ol' porch to enjoy the dripping of breakup.

"C'mon Honey! The sun's going down. We'll sit outside for a while and watch the icicles refreeze before we go to bed."

The opportunity to enjoy an exciting and fulfilling outside, spingtime activity like that raises havoc with the TV ratings, no doubt.

Summer isn't the time when Alaskans need to save daylight. We're talking Land of the Midnight Sun here, remember? With nineteen to twenty-four hours of daylight, if the need for more daylight is felt during the summer months, there is a definite need to cut back on the caffeine consumption.

The October switch is just the opposite. Just when we really do need the extra hour of daylight in the evenings (normally to finish up all those things that should have been done before the sun headed south for the winter), the time changers short us.

"What are you doing, Dear?"

"I'm picking up after the dog."

"It's awfully dark. Can you see?"

"I'm doing it by feel. Oh, yuck..."

What advantages are there to the time changes? Well, we're still an hour behind the West Coast, and four hours behind the East Coast. And then there's all those candles we're saving. Let's not forget that.

Ol' Sparky

I have given up watching most television. I firmly believe that it leads to severe mental atrophy. Even so, every now and then something will catch my attention as I walk past the TV while the kids are watching. More often than not, it's a commercial. I think the best entertainment available to the viewers today is to be found in television commercials. The one ad that invariably breaks me up is for a brand of coffee. It's the one where an attractive, young couple is happily sipping away a relaxing cup of java in front of a beautiful fire. It is that sort of romanticized glop the uninformed envision when they think of heating with wood. I know we did.

When the Realtor showed us what was to become our castle, the words "all electric" slid glibly from her lips. My wife had seen an episode of *Lifestyles of the Obscenely, Disgustingly, Filthy Rich* where the subject had actually used electric heat one month, and voiced some concern. The Realtor was ready for the challenge by calmly explaining that there was a fireplace in the living room, and a wood stove in the rec-room downstairs. That was all it took: free heat in the form of readily accessible wood. We plunked down earnest money right then and there.

Here's a tip for house hunters: the price you offer for a home with wood heat will not ensure the availability of any fuel for your fireplace and/or wood-burning stove. The day we moved in, it was disappointing to discover that one small shred of water soaked birch bark was the sum total of our wood supply. Our celebratory fire was limited to the kitchen matches on hand, and that first cup of coffee had the distinct flavor of sulfur to it.

In order to reap the benefits of all the free heat, I found it necessary to make a few initial investments: an axe, a wedge, a maul, and of course, a chainsaw.

It would have been counterproductive to spend a great deal of money assembling the tools needed to collect all that free heat, so a good deal was made on a used chainsaw. There are two things I now know beyond certainty that should never be purchased used: toothpicks and chainsaws.

A card hanging up at the post office put me in touch with the owner of a used chainsaw who was willing to part with it for the paltry sum of fifty dollars. It wasn't merely old, it was a remnant of antiquity. It had been made, I would guess, a couple of decades before whipsaws went out of fashion. There were, as the seller proudly pointed out, "No cheap plastic parts on that baby. It's *all* metal! And none of those darn safety features to slow you down, neither. 'Course, I did put on one of them anti- kickback bars to keep the missus happy."

The anti-kickback bar he was referring to was a piece of pipe that had been bent and attached to the handle by means of hose clamps and duct tape. It appeared as though it was perfectly positioned to snap your arm in two just above the wrist in the event of a stout kickback.

It was readily apparent that if I didn't jump at this opportunity immediately, someone from the Smithsonian was going to breeze in and snatch it out from under me. After a quick demonstration, the deal was done.

"Kind of hate to see ol' Sparky go. She's got a few little quirks, but that chainsaw's cut more trees than most folks ever see. Tell you what, if you want it to start easy, keep her in the house. She's kinda cold blooded."

The next morning, the first of ol' Sparky's quirks became known: she was apparently the first of the automatic chain oilers, and the feature was not at all dependent upon the chain moving. With a quick clean up and an oil reservoir refill, it was time to make sawdust.

It was a crisp October morning, and the beads of sweat didn't appear until I had pulled on the starter rope for twenty minutes. It was time to call the seller.

"Did ya do like I said, and keep her inside?"

I affirmed that Sparky had been most comfortable all night, dribbling oil on the rug by the back door.

"Ya didn't try an start her outside did ya?"

"Well, yes. You mean it needs to be started inside?"

"Yep. Betcha used full choke too. Can't do that. She don't want to get up an' go fast first thing in the morning. Gotta start her slow. Just a little quirk of hers. Probably dribblin' gas out the exhaust. You're lucky she didn't fire off. Coulda blown yourself up. Bring her in to dry out and try it again in a few hours. Bye."

A few hours later, ol' Sparky roared to life with enough force to cause our cat to ricochet out of the room, leaving great tufts of fur floating in the currents of her departure. (We later had to relocate the litter box to the other side of the house, as the stress of returning to that room caused most of the remaining hair to also drop out.)

With Sparky snarling ominously, we made our way to a beetle killed spruce on the back side of the lot to begin the "Nikiski Chainsaw Massacre." Great hordes of small woodland creatures fled in panic before us.

Judging the direction of lean, I made the wedge cut, then turned Sparky over for the final cut. Suddenly, the only sound was the ringing in my ears. A quick jerk on the rope and Sparky was back in business, but only until I tipped her on her side again. Time to call the seller.

"I'll bet she quit when you rolled her on her right side. Can't do that."

"You mean she'll only cut on the left?"

"No, she cuts good up an' down too, but she won't run when you tip her to the right more'n about twenty degrees. Just one of them quirks. You'll get the hang of it. Bye."

Back to the massacre, which developed into more of a woodland ballet as I danced around trying to keep ol' Sparky running.

With three trees down, it was time to cut splitting lengths. Lining up for a straight cut, the bar started in and slowly cut an arc, rolling Sparky to the right. Time to call the seller.

"Look down that bar. See how it's sorta creased? That happened when a big ol' birch sorta spun and pinched it. I'd say ya oughta get a new bar, but they don't make em' like that anymore. I got the last one, that one, 'bout fifteen years ago."

"So how do I get more than halfway through a log!?"

"Well, ya cut in from the left and let 'er roll straight. Your angle depends on how thick the log is. Just one of them quirks. You'll get the hang of it. Bye."

It didn't take much more than the rest of the weekend to get the hang of it, but splitting lengths that rolled over on one end and leaned over on the other, was more than I could master. Time to call the seller.

"Well, I don't really need two chainsaws, but I'll take her back and give you a cord of unsplit firewood. You want to buy more than that too, it's seventy a cord."

"Okay, you've got a deal, I'll take six cords. What'll you do with ol' Sparky?"

"Oh, I s'pose I'll sell her to somebody with all electric heat next fall. Just one of them quirks."

I finally got the hang of it.

Cup of Coffee

The shadows grow longer every day as the daily dose of sun grows shorter. The clear nights bring on frost. We are passing through that short span of time referred to as fall. The frantic pace of summer is over. It is now time to kick back and prepare to settle into the slower routine of winter.

Winter. Responses to that word vary from simple quiet moans to cacophonous wailings and gnashing of teeth. Any attempted discussion of winter at this time of year will cause immediate knee jerk attempts to change the subject in vain attempts to stave off the inevitable.

"Whooee, baby! Sure got cold last night. Winter's on the way."

"Honey, would you please go check the fuchsias to see if they need watering?"

"The frost killed 'em a week ago."

"No, they're just a little droopy from lack of water."

"Sweetheart, they are deader than a *hammer*."

"*Water the damn fuchsias!*"

"I can't. The hose is frozen."

Just ignoring winter won't improve the situation. One must develop an attitude of at least acceptance, or winter will stretch into an interminable period of depression, broken only by lighter periods of sullen gloom. Even better than plain acceptance is developing an enthusiasm for winter.

This is the approach my neighbor, "Blizzard Bob" (B.B.) has taken. B.B. embraces winter with an enthusiasm that could best be described as rabid. The man aches for the first snow, and the opportunity to crank up his turbo-charged Belchflame Spewmaster snowthrower. He literally cheers when the borough snow plows leave chest high berms at the end of his drive. His maniacal laugh echoes through the neighborhood when the dark of winter moves to a shade of blindness with a heavy snow. He is the hairy legged Pollyanna of the frozen north.

What could possibly prompt an individual to express such glee in the face of such adversity? A caffeine induced surrealistic perception of the world brought about by massive amounts of coffee, and the knowledge that in all probability, everyone is home with little or no chance of escape.

B.B. fancies himself as the Kenai Peninsula's own coffee gourmet extraordinaire. There is not a single type of coffee bean available to the buying public that B.B. has not tried, and in most cases, made an attempt to improve upon by blending in some fashion.

This passion has its drawbacks. Being a purist, B.B. won't deal with decaffeinated beans.

"You can't tell me that it tastes the same. I don't care how they do it. If you take the caffeine out of the bean you're gonna take the heart out of the blend."

Bob's wife has confided that at the height of winter, when B.B. is at the peak of his experimental blends, he doesn't really sleep. She says he simply passes out for brief periods of time, twitching restlessly, every third or fourth day, depending on the strength of the blend he happens to be working on at the time.

Winter is the season of socialization for B.B., because he knows Alaskans are a lot like birds: we scatter to attend our own affairs during the summer, and group together to pass the winter in company. Only, instead of a berry bush, we congregate around a coffee pot.

When the wind snaps like a whip against your face, and the scenery is a bleak, black and white abstract, quiet conversation steeped in the aroma of a freshly brewed pot of coffee warms the soul as much as the body. That is, until the galloping grind gourmet shows up pounding on the door, like he did one unforgettable evening last winter.

"Hello in there! It's me, Bob. Hello? C'mon guys, I know you're in there. I can see the cars, I know you're home. How 'bout a cup of coffee?"

Since the presence of the cars was a dead give away, and the continued pounding would have only stopped conversation anyway, B.B. was let in. He whirled into the room like a hyper dust devil. His hollow, sunken, bloodshot eyes were frozen open in testimony of his latest quest for the ultimate coffee bean blend. He carried a little paper bag clutched tightly to his chest. His nose wrinkled immediately upon smelling our fresh coffee.

"Whew! You boiling tar or what? Oh no, just some of that canned coffee. Well, have I got a treat for you."

"Good to see you too B.B., want a cup of fresh coffee?"

"Don't mind if I do. I'll brew it up right away. Brought a new special blend with me just so you could try it out. First I gotta wash the pot and the basket. Can't leave any old oils to taint the flavor of this special blend. Where's the dish soap?"

Turned loose with the dish soap, he scrubbed feverishly on the pot and basket to remove the last miniscule traces of any offending residue. "Where's your distilled water?"

"I'm ashamed to admit it, but I don't have any."

"Fine then," he was obviously put out, "but you should know that the coffee's only as good as the water it's made with. My blend here can't brew up to its full potential..."

"Whoa there B.B., I don't want to hold back any potential here. Maybe we ought to put this off until some other time when I've got the right water."

"No, no. We'll make do for now. Just so long as you know that what's good with this nasty ol' tap water would have been just this side of celestial with good water. Just keep that in mind."

With the admonishment finished, he opened the little paper bag with trembling, caffeine generated excitement, and shakily measured exactly three scoops with his special brass "blend spoon" into the special, unbleached, acid free filter he'd brought along.

"Say B.B., what're all those red and white specks in the grinds there?"

He just smiled slyly, "That's what makes it so special. Just wait."

As all present waited for the water to drip and the blend to weave its magic, B.B. launched into his patented lecture on different beans and what makes them flavorful.

"And with that in mind, I chose the French roast for exactly that lightly burned acrid touch, and the Columbian because of the more mellow, aromatic quality. Then, I stepped into realms of blending heretofore never explored... but wait! Ahh... smell the essence of blending genius."

B.B. grabbed the carafe just as the coffeemaker sputtered out its last gasp of steam, and quickly poured each person a cup of the new ambrosia. "Quick, what do you think? Nectar of the gods, or what?"

Tightly pursed lips on silent, tilted, squinty-eyed faces offered no response. Finally, one taster after another swallowed hard.

B.B. listened intently to the first review.

"Well, it's different. Sorta salty."

"Wait a minute," another taste tester interrupted, "what's wrong with your lips there?"

"Probably the same thing as yours. Stick out your tongue. Omigosh! Are you bleeding?"

"No, if I was bleeding the salt would tell me from exactly where. What gives B.B.?"

Obviously, something was amiss. The taste test had serious side effects. B.B. looked shocked, and finally stam-mered out that the red dye was from the secret ingredient. "You have been treated to my special new blend: French-Columbian-Pistachio delight."

"Pistachios? The red stain is from Pistachios? You used the *shells*?"

B.B. tried to explain, "I was up all last night perfecting it, didn't get it just so until after noon today. It tasted so good, I brewed and drank everything I'd blended. I knew you'd want to try this, so I made some more. Problem is, by then I was shakin' so bad I couldn't hold onto the pistachios to shell 'em, so I just ground 'em up with the beans. I mean, what's the harm? The shells stay in the filter. Right?"

There was no chance for an answer, as at that point, B.B. took one of his impromptu naps.

I'm not sure what B.B. will do for company this winter. We've all switched to tea in this neighborhood.

The SAT
(Standardized Alaskan Test)

One of the things that sets Alaskans apart from people located elsewhere in the country (other than record club memberships, car insurance and nationally broadcast radio commercials with exclusionary statements that make all sales offers null and void) is our attitude toward life and how we deal with situations that are unique to life in our area. The attitudes and actions associated with living here are learned through examples set by others. Gaining them can take years. Sometimes, new residents and visitors feel awkward when they aren't quite sure how to react, and lose the pleasure of the moment just trying to blend in.

Most of the awkward or embarrassing feelings that people feel could be eliminated if there was some easy way to train for the new and unfamiliar Alaskan situations. What is needed is some sort of study guide to be distributed by the Department of Tourism, various Chambers of Commerce and local information booths. That way, in the privacy of their own homes, hotel rooms or recreational vehicles, newcomers of all sorts could prepare to really get out and enjoy Alaska by being Alaskan. What is needed is an SAT (Standardized Alaskan Test), a self guided, learn at your own pace, study course.

We've all seen this kind of program advertised before. The covers on matchbooks offer similar training all the time: "Earn a Doctorate in nuclear physics in the privacy of your own home, and at your own pace!" If you haven't seen that one, perhaps you've caught the one about the promising future that could be yours after just a few home study lessons in neurosurgery. At any rate, I don't see why a similar approach wouldn't work for folks that want to get an edge on becoming more Alaskan.

This concept could even be useful as a guidance tool for people that are thinking about moving up here. The state could run a nationwide advertising campaign in newspapers across the country: "Prepared for Alaska? Take the SAT and see. Send one dollar now, plus six-thirty-seven for postage and handling, and see if you've got what it takes." I realize the postage and handling charges may seem a little steep, but the state needs the revenue.

The test works this way: a real life situation is described, and several possible responses are described. You are to pick the best response for the situation. Since the explanations are provided at the end of the question for reference only, you are on your honor to review the explanations only after having selected a response.

Standardized Alaskan Test

SITUATION: You and a friend are driving to town on a road that is coated with glare ice (black ice). A light, wet snow has started to fall, making the road even more slick than it was when your trip began. You turn to your friend and say:

A) Let's go back home and wait until the road is sanded.

B) Geez, I hope a moose doesn't step out in front of me, I don't think I could stop.

C) Let's set the parking brake and see if we can slide all the way to town.

D) I'm not worried, I've got four wheel drive; no way we'll slide off.

EXPLANATION: Answer A is wrong; if Alaskans waited for the roads to be sanded every time they got bad, they'd never go anywhere. Answer B is wrong; an Alaskan would *know* there would be no chance of stopping. Answer D is wrong; Alaskans use four-wheel drive primarily to get out of the ditch. Answer C is correct; Alaskans love a sporting challenge.

SITUATION: It is the first part of August, in an even numbered year. You and a friend, who just moved up less than a year ago, are fishing on the Kenai River. The pink salmon are in thick enough to walk on. Your friend is having the time of his life. You tell him:

A) I'm going home, no point in even trying to get anything worthwhile with all the humpies around.

B) Go ahead and fish, I'll just watch.

C) Humpies are pretty good eating when they're fresh.

D) I don't like to waste my time on humpies, but I need the eggs.

EXPLANATION: Answer A is wrong; an Alaskan would never give up without being forced to release at least twenty of those nasty pinks first. Answer B is wrong; that is a physical impossibility. Answer C is wrong; they are, but an Alaskan wouldn't admit having tried them. Answer D is correct, but you won't fool anybody.

SITUATION: You are standing in the check out line of a food store when the whole building begins to shake. You:

A) Quickly move to a doorway.

B) Firmly hold on to your shopping basket.

C) Shout, "Earthquake!"

D) None of the above.

EXPLANATION: Answer A is incorrect; you would lose your place in line if you ran for a doorway. Answer B is wrong; although shopping baskets are some of the world's most immovable objects, they wouldn't help when the earth is moving. Answer C is wrong; why make a declaration of the obvious? Answer D is correct; most of the time you're too surprised (and scared) to do anything deliberate anyway.

SITUATION: The people of Alaska decided to preserve some of the wealth generated by oil revenues in the form of a Permanent Fund to insure that the State legislators didn't simply fritter it away. Each year, a portion of the earnings from that fund are disbursed to residents. You have resided in Alaska long enough to qualify for a Permanent Fund Dividend. When you receive the check, you immediately:

A) Purchase a ticket for Hawaii.

B) Set it aside to provide for your children's education.
C) Use the check for the down payment on a new home.
D) Invest it in a mutual fund.
EXPLANATION: This is a "gimme" question. One need not look beyond answer A.

SITUATION: You want to take the family out camping and get away for a relaxing Memorial Day weekend. You should plan to go:
A) To the Anchor River.
B) To the Homer Spit.
C) To Anchorage.
D) To the Kasilof River.
EXPLANATION: Answer C is the correct answer, provided you enjoy visiting ghost towns. Answers A, B and D are incorrect, as they list waters open to king salmon fishing.

SITUATION: After having planted your new lawn in the front yard, you should protect the seedlings by:
A) Erecting a scarecrow.
B) Placing a rope fence around the perimeter.
C) Planting a garden in the back yard.
D) None of the above.
EXPLANATION: Answer A is incorrect; unless you're growing tin cans or French fries, the staples of Alaskan ravens. Answer B is wrong; rope fences won't stop anything: kids climb on them and moose step right over. Answer C is incorrect; a garden acts as moose magnet, the resulting divots stomped into your lawn from the ensuing stampede will prevent anything worthwhile from growing, ever. Answer D is the correct answer; there is absolutely nothing that will protect a lawn from complete and total destruction. Don't even try it, just stick to fishing in the summer.

SITUATION: You have heard rumors of substantial budget cuts in state services for the borough. You want to hear all the facts. You should:
A) Contact the state agencies involved.
B) Call your State representative.
C) Contact your State senator.

D) Go rent a video.

EXPLANATION: Answer A is incorrect; don't call them until you have something to pass along. Answer B and C are wrong; you are looking for facts. Answer D is correct; take your time in selecting a movie, listen in on the conversations, and in less than thirty minutes you'll have enough facts to follow through with Answer A.

SITUATION: Your house needs some exterior work: a little painting, perhaps a little shingling, some new siding. When is the best time to do the needed repairs?
A) In the spring.
B) Next Summer.
C) Between salmon runs.
D) As soon as possible.

EXPLANATION: Answer A is incorrect; spring is not a good time to work on a home, because much time is needed to ensure a proper preventive maintenance program on all the summer gear you will be using, such as the boat, the camper, etc. Answer C is silly; by the time the preventive maintenance program is completed, the kings are running, then the reds, followed by the silvers, and they run right up until late fall when it's too cold to do anything except go hunting and ice fishing. Answer D is not practical; repairs take time to plan out. A rushed job is a sloppy job. Answer B is correct; any repairs should *always* be done "next summer." Example: We will finish painting the house "next summer," just as we have planned each year for the past five years.

SITUATION: In the past three weeks, your neighbor's dog has gotten into your garbage four or five times. Even when the garbage cans are sealed, the dog will knock them over, and proceed to strew the contents all around your yard. You should:
A) Explain the situation to your neighbor, and ask that the dog be confined.
B) Shoot the dog.
C) Clean the old, freezer burned fish out of your freezer.
D) Move.

EXPLANATION: Answer A is wrong; you will have undoubtedly accused the wrong culprit as, "My dog wouldn't do anything like that!" Answer B is incorrect; although it might sound tempting, an act of violence against a dog that is just acting normal is foolish, and will do nothing to maintain any sort of civility with the neighbor. Answer D is wrong; with the housing market like it is, the dog will die of old age before you could sell. Answer C is the correct answer; not only will you accomplish something constructive, if you let the fish thaw for a day or two before throwing them out, the dog will have something to roll in, and the neighbor will have a good reason to confine the dog.

SITUATION: It is the Christmas season, and you are going to set up your tree. What is the best way to avoid getting a carpet full of spruce needles?

A) Select and cut a tree as close to your home as possible.
B) Soak the freshly cut tree in sugar water before putting it in the tree stand, and water it daily.
C) Cut the tree and put it up on Christmas Eve.
D) None of the above.

EXPLANATION: Answer A is wrong; cutting the tree close to home will shorten the travel time, thereby reducing the number of already loose needles that are bumped, knocked, blown, scraped, or pulled off. Answer B is incorrect; this is a trick, one of those "sounds good in theory" practices. Answer C is incorrect; this too, is a good idea in theory, but there is some sort of inexplicable natural phenomenon that occurs at the stroke of midnight on Christmas Eve that causes any spruce tree inside, no matter how fresh, to drop all its needles. Answer D is correct; there isn't a darn thing that can be done (except using an artificial tree... bleah!) to prevent getting spruce needles in the carpet.

SITUATION: You had to have a real, cut it yourself Christmas tree. You now have a carpet full of needles. You should:

A) Throw a party.
B) Steam clean the carpet.
C) Vacuum the carpet several times with a beater bar.
D) Rearrange the furniture to cover the area where the tree dropped all the needles.

EXPLANATION: Answer B is incorrect; steam cleaning spruce needles merely melts them to the fibers (it does smell nice though). Answer C is wrong; you can beater bar the carpet to a frazzle, and you will simply create fuzz with spruce needles in it. Answer D is incorrect; this is only a temporary solution, as spruce needles "creep" through the nap until found by a bare foot. Answer A is correct; each guest is to pick as many spruce needles from the carpet as possible, the person with the most needles at the end of the evening wins a door prize such as a trip for two to Hawaii. (Nobody would do it for free.)

SITUATION: It is the 24th of April. The roads are clear of ice and snow. Alaska law requires that studded tires be removed by May 1st. You have studded tires on your vehicle. You should:

A) Have your spare set of summer tires mounted as soon as possible to avoid the last minute rush.

B) Wait until the last moment to have summer tires mounted and get in line with everyone else.

C) Pull the studs out of the tires yourself.

D) Forget about it.

EXPLANATION: Answer A is incorrect. If you take your vehicle in to have the tires changed out before April 30th, everyone in the service station will *know* you are a newcomer. If you chose answer B, you have your seasons switched. Alaskans wait until the last possible moment (usually after being pulled from a ditch) to mount the studded winter tires. Answer C is also incorrect. A person can remove the studs by popping them out with a thin screwdriver, but you'll never get new studs back in after the holes fill with grit. Answer D is what real Alaskans do without even thinking about it.

SITUATION: With the longer, warmer days, the snow is melting off at a rapid rate. Most of the side roads are not much more than well traveled, muddy sloughs. Your car is covered with an even coat of grime. You should:

A) Wait until past break-up before washing the vehicle.

B) Wash the grime off at least once a week.

C) Drive only on dry roads.

D) None of the above.

EXPLANATION: Answer A seems to be the logical answer, but as soon as break-up is over, it's time to hit the back trails to the fishing holes. Why waste the effort? Answer B indicates one of two things: either you are a transplanted Californian, or you are anal compulsive, which is almost as bad. If you chose answer C, this is your first break-up. Answer D is correct, because Alaskans know the only real protection against a dulled finish is to keep the car covered with a thick protective coating of grime.

SITUATION: As the snow melts away, your lawn is nothing but a compressed mat of dead thatch. You should:

A) Get out there while it's still damp and rake up the dead thatch to keep mold from growing.

B) Wait for it to dry out and burn it off.

C) Ignore the lawn, and plan your summer excursions.

D) Do both A and B, to return necessary nutrients to the soil, and allow the new grass to grow more rapidly.

EXPLANATION: Answer A is incorrect. What's a little mold? It's not as if anyone is driving around looking at lawns this time of year. Answer B is fun, but it makes your shoes smell funny. Answer D is definitely the wrong answer. If you do all that to your lawn, your neighbors are going to feel obligated to do the same. Do you *really* want to alienate your neighbors? Answer C is correct. Ignoring your lawn now will prevent massive amounts of work later. Develop good lawn abuse habits early to ensure a carefree summer.

SITUATION: As an individual that enjoys fishing (read that as fishaholic), the melting snow, running water and warmer weather have you pretty much worked into a lather. To relieve the symptoms, you should:

A) Rent a video on fishing.

B) Go window shopping at the local sporting goods stores.

C) Make a list of things that need to be done around the house.

D) Clean your tackle box.

EXPLANATION: Renting a video on fishing during break-up is like treating a sunburn with Ben-Gay. Answer A is not simply wrong, it's dangerous. Answer B is silly. Who ever heard of an Alaskan fisherman "window shopping" in a sporting goods store? This is not only incorrect, but probably impossible. Answer D separates those that merely casually pursue fish and those that are consumed with the flames of passion over the quest for fish: tackle boxes are never cleaned by the latter, and the former don't have a problem waiting out break-up. Answer C is the correct answer. Making such a list will not only take your mind off fishing, but will give you an early start in developing ironclad excuses for not doing those things during fishing season.

SITUATION: A relative in the Lower Forty-eight calls and starts talking about all their warm weather, flowers, green grass and so forth. In response, you should:

    A) Scream a long list of epithets and hang up.

EXPLANATION: This is a "gimme," as there isn't any other answer that could even remotely seem feasible.

SITUATION: It seems plain wasteful to you to buy your children break-up boots. They will only wear them for a few short weeks at most, and then outgrow them before next year. What should be your course of action?

    A)   Not buy any at all.

    B)   Buy break-up boots three sizes too big for your child.

    C)   Look for used, cheaply priced break-up boots at garage sales, thrift shops and so forth.

    D)   Show concern for your child's well-being and buy break-up boots in the child's exact shoe size.

EXPLANATION: If you selected answer A, shame on you! Do you want to deprive your child of the Alaskan tradition of clumping around as if he or she had cement blocks for feet while whining about "these stupid boots?" Answer C is incorrect. Looking for serviceable, used break-up boots is tantamount to the quest for the Holy Grail. The name "break-up boot" refers to what they do. The fact that the season they are used in is also referred to as break-up is merely coincidental. Answer D is wrong: see the following explanation for why. Answer B is the correct answer. Buying break-up boots three sizes too big has nothing to do with being able to use them the following year. These boots are designed in such a manner that socks will be stripped from the wearer's foot within three steps. In order to protect your child from pinched toes, plenty of room for the sock to migrate must be provided.

SITUATION: You want to supplement your heat with wood. What is the best way to ensure an adequate supply?

A) Order your wood in July.

B) Order your wood in August.

C) Order your wood in September.

D) Order your wood in late October, after the first heavy snowfall.

EXPLANATION: Answer A is incorrect: your order will be lost and/or forgotten during the frenzy of the fishing season. Answer B is incorrect: nobody has time to deliver wood in August, they're getting ready for moose season. Answer C is incorrect: you will not be able to order wood in September, because everyone is out hunting. Answer D is the correct answer: due to the fire hazards associated with wood, it is a law that firewood can't be delivered before it is covered with ice and snow, or dumped onto a snow covered patch of ground that will prevent the spread of any resultant fire. This extra protection means that the price of firewood will be higher than what was advertised earlier, when you couldn't get it.

SITUATION: A man shows up at your house with a truck that has a plow on it, and offers to put you on a route to plow your drive for the winter. The service would cost twenty-five dollars a clearing. You should:

A) Offer him twenty dollars a clearing.

B) Insist on a written contract.

C) Call the police or troopers.

D) Look around for a better deal.

EXPLANATION: Answer C is the only correct answer. The man is either demented, casing your home for a burglary, or even worse, trying to get into the house to make a magazine sales pitch. The price is the best tip: nobody charges less than thirty dollars a clearing. The only way to get the kind of service this man is offering, and only then at a substantially higher price, is to have a close relative die and leave the option to you in a will.

SITUATION: You are on a tight budget, and your child has just informed you that they want to play hockey. You should:

A) Immediately go out and purchase an expensive pair of hockey skates and a good set of pads.

B) Purchase an inexpensive pair of hockey skates and pads.

C) Wait and talk to the coach.

D) Quit your job, give up your house and move to Arizona.

EXPLANATION: Answer D is the correct answer: it is cheaper than answer A, which is exactly what the coach in answer C will tell you to do. Answer B doesn't exist in the real world.

SITUATION: Your house is located half a mile off the main road. Early one morning, you look out the window to see that a huge storm has deposited over two feet of snow in the night. The snow looks too deep for your car to go through, but you hear snow plows headed your way. You should:

A) Call work immediately to leave the message that you'll be a little late.

B) Continue sleeping.

C) Go outside and see if the snowplow has already been by before calling work.

D) Get ready for work before checking to see if the road has been plowed.

EXPLANATION: Answers A, C and D are incorrect. The only correct action in this situation is to continue sleeping, because you have dreamed the entire affair. If a storm passed through in the course of the night, leaving behind two feet of snow, the snowplows wouldn't be on the secondary roads until at least the next day.

SITUATION: You have a set of studded snow tires for your vehicle. When should you make arrangements to have them mounted?

A) As the tow truck is hooking up to pull you from the ditch.

B) As soon as it is legal.

C) No later than the first week of November.

D) After the first heavy snow.

EXPLANATION: Answers B and C are incorrect, as there is no way to judge the correct, specific date to put on snow tires. If the studded tires are run too long on dry pavement, the studs are ground down to nothing. Answer D is incorrect, but can lead us to the correct answer, which is answer A. Not only have you determined that it is an appropriate time to have the tires mounted and prevented unnecessary wear on your studs, you have ensured that your mechanic is available at the exact moment you want your tires mounted. Now is the time to work out a primo deal on a tow and tire mounting package. (You smart shopper.)

SITUATION: You want to clear a path through your mudroom (or arctic entry). Which of the following will be useful in the coming months, and should not be moved to an inaccessible location? (There may be more than one answer)
A) A plastic bladed snow shovel with a specially designed ergonomic handle.
B) A push broom.
C) A garden trowel.
D) A gas powered lawn trimmer.

EXPLANATION: A push broom is handy for shoving snow off your vehicle, so answer B is correct. Garden trowels are the perfect size to get into wheel wells to dig out packed in snow, and can be used to spread kitty litter on icy walks, so answer C is correct. Answer D is also correct: nothing beats the reach and efficiency of a gas powered lawn trimmer in removing those really troublesome, hard to reach icicles. The plastic blade that bends and/or breaks upon use, and the back strain inducing "ergonomic" handle of the snow shovel in answer A make it the only incorrect answer.

YOU AND YOUR SCORE: If you answered only the even numbers correctly, it means you got every other answer right. If you answered only the odd numbers correctly, you got about half right.

If you answered them all correctly, you probably cheat at cards too.

SPECIAL BONUS QUESTION:
SITUATION: You have just finished the SAT. You did not score well. You should:
A) Leave or not visit Alaska.
B) Retake the test.
C) Vow to read everything you can find about Alaska.
D) Think to yourself, "What a stupid test! What does that Bozo know anyway?"

EXPLANATION: None needed if you chose answer D.

The End

Thanks for reading *Of Moose and Men.* If you have any comments, suggestions or corrections we'd like to hear from you. You can send e-mail directly to the author at aegcp@ptialaska.net. Written comments can be mailed to: OMM Books, P.O. Box 7397, Nikiski, AK 99635

Order Form

Why steal the library's or your friend's copy when you can get your very own *Of Moose and Men* copy for only $12.95 plus shipping? A great deal at twice the price. (Oh, all right, you'd be really ripped if we charged you twice the price, but at least you'd be honest.) To stay honest, fill out this form and mail it with a check or money order to:

> **OMM Books**
> **P.O. Box 7397**
> **Nikiski, AK 99635**

Oh, be still my beating heart! I want to order _____ copies at $12.95 each, plus $2.00 for US Post Office book rate shipping on each book ordered (for a total of 14.95 for each book).

Number of books _____ X $14.95 = $ _____ total due

Please send my order to:

Name _____

Address _____

City _____

State and Zip _____

Thank you for your order

Please note: Books shipped by US Postal book rate can take up to four weeks for delivery. If you want your shipment to go priority mail, please enclose an extra $2.00 ($16.95 per book total).